SECRET
SEVILLE

Ricardo de Castro

JONGLEZ PUBLISHING

Travel guides

A social psychologist by profession, and expert in environmental subjects, Ricardo de Castro has been living in Seville for more than 35 years. He has always been interested in discovering the stories, places and secrets of the city on the banks of the Guadalquivir, where surprising oddities spring out of every nook and cranny. His interests also take in literature, contemporary art and ethnic music, and he has a particularly open mind when it comes to the world around us, leading him to work as a travel guide in a range of destinations including France, Italy, Morocco, Tunisia, Slovenia and Turkey.

It has been our great pleasure to compile this guide to *Secret Seville*, and we hope readers will find it just as useful for discovering unusual, hidden and hitherto unknown sides of the city as we have. The descriptions of some of the locations include information boxes with historical aspects and anecdotal accounts, providing a greater insight into the city in all its complexity.

Secret Seville uncovers numerous details about many of the places we walk past every day without even noticing them. They are an invitation to take a closer look at the urban landscape and, in a more general sense, a way of discovering our city with the same curiosity and enthusiasm with which we travel to other places ...

We welcome any comments you might have about the guide, or information about places not mentioned in it. This will help us to complete future editions.

Do not hesitate to write to us at:
- Jonglez Publishing,
  25, rue du Maréchal Foch,
  78000 Versailles, France
- Email: info@jonglezpublishing.com

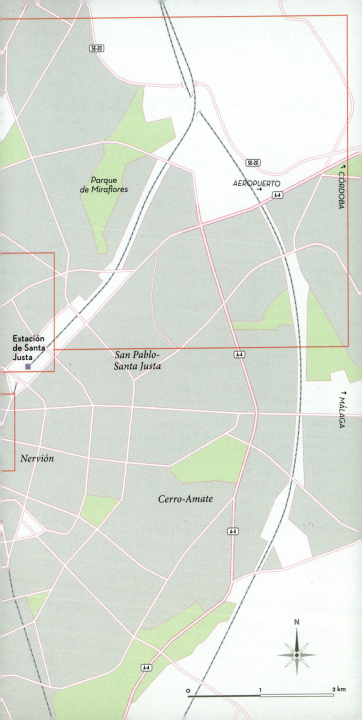

SE-20

Parque
de Miraflores

SE-20

AEROPUERTO
→ A-4

↑ CÓRDOBA

A-4

Estación
de Santa
Justa

San Pablo-
Santa Justa

↑ MÁLAGA

Nervión

Cerro-Amate

A-4

A-4

N

A-4

0   1   2 km

CONTENT

Alameda, San Vicente and San Julián

Centro, Alfalfa and Museo

Santa Cruz, Cathedral and San Bartolomé

CONTENT

Triana and Los Remedios

Puerta de Jerez and Avenida de la Palmera

Cartuja Island and San Jerónimo

Alameda, San Vicente and San Julián

HORSE'S HEAD
AT THE GARAJE LAVERÁN

An early 20th-century transport emporium

Calle Goles, 44

Over the garage door of a building on the corner of Calle Goles and Calle Baños you'll see the curious bust of a horse's head framed by a medallion.

This unusual decorative feature recalls what was, in times long past, the famous Laverán Garage, which started off as a factory producing horse-drawn coaches and later became a carriage-hire and parking business.

The modernist building was constructed between 1912 and 1913 by architect Aurelio Gómez Millán. Its central nave was designed to house a 19th-century iron structure apparently built by a disciple of Gustave Eiffel.

The original factory was set up by a Frenchman from Toulouse called Antonio Laveran y Mandement, who, after completing his studies in Paris, moved to the Andalusian capital to set up a horse-drawn coach factory.

Laveran was a great entrepreneur, a friend of Picasso and Winston Churchill, and his business evolved into a luxury gala carriage rental service – prices varied according to the number of horses, hours of use and number of passengers.

In 1914 Laveran set up the first franchise in the city as a representative of the French manufacturer De Dion-Bouton, the most important global automobile brand of its day.

Over time, the Laverán Garage was used as parking for motor vehicles until it finally closed in 2004, having been run by four generations of the same family. It is currently used as a depot for archaeological pieces from the Seville City Council collection.

WEEPING STONE

A lament for young firing-squad victims

Calle San Laureano, 7

Very close to where the Puerta Real (Royal Gateway) used to stand, at the foot of the old convent that later became the San Laureano barracks, you'd be forgiven for not noticing an unprepossessing stone block. Only elderly locals still call it by its name: *la piedra llorosa* (the

weeping stone). Here, it is said, sat García de Vinuesa (who became mayor a year later), overcome with remorse at having been unable to save 82 sons of the city from the firing squad.

In 1857, during the reign of Queen Isabella II, there was an uprising involving a group of young progressive liberals under the command of Joaquín Serra (a retired colonel) and Manuel Caro. Serra had fought in the Carlist Wars and was exiled from Spain on several occasions because of his democratic and republican beliefs. Under his leadership, the group set out for Ronda, hoping to stir up the support of other Andalusian towns. The uprising gained momentum in the towns of El Arahal and Utrera (both in the Seville area), where the peasants rose up against the system of land ownership and the high cost of living. In response, the government sent in the military and, having caught up with the rebels, killed 25 of them despite their lack of resistance, taking the survivors prisoner.

Back in Seville, they were locked up in the San Laureano barracks; a few days later it was decided that the 82 prisoners would face the firing squad, though none of them had committed crimes of violence. Despite pleas for mercy on the part of the City Council, the executions took place in Plaza de Armas at the Campo de Marte, where the old train station still stands today.

NEARBY
Remains of the Puerta Real ③
Corner of Plaza Puerta Real and Calle San Laureano

Only a small section of the Almohad wall remains at the Puerta Real: you'll see a stone plaque that was originally found on its façade. This piece of marble commemorates the reconstruction of the gateway in 1564 by order of Philip II – a few years later, he passed under it on entering the city. This explains why its original name of Puerta de Goles (a possible distortion of the name Hercules) was changed. A sculpture of the mythical hero, standing at the top, is believed to have been moved at the same time. The demolition of Seville's medieval walls and gates started when García de Vinuesa was mayor, with the Puerta Real disappearing for ever in 1864.

MURAL OF THE TROOPS OF CHARLES V

A spectacular ceramic panel from 1906

Plaza del Museo, 6

Hidden at the entrance to a noble mansion opposite the Museo de Bellas Artes (Museum of Fine Arts), you'll see an enormous ceramic panel dating from the early 20th century. This is a faithful reproduction of a 1554 tapestry commissioned by Charles V entitled *Review of the Troops at Barcelona*.

This spectacular 3-metre-high mural was executed in 1906 by artist Manuel Rodríguez Pérez de Tudela, using the flat painted tile technique. It was initially installed at the Salinas palace, opposite the church of Santa Cruz, as was the panel opposite it: *The Surrender of Granada*, executed one year later by the same artist and based on a work by Francisco Pradilla Ortiz in the Palacio del Senado (Senate Palace).

Both pieces were purchased in the 1990s by art collector Mariano Bellver, who installed them at the entranceway leading to the spectacular patio of his home in Plaza del Museo.

The mural shows Emperor Charles V inspecting the troops as they prepare to embark from the port of Barcelona in 1535 to undertake an expedition against the feared pirate Hayreddin Barbarossa, a Turkish corsair serving the Ottoman Sultan Suleiman I. Barbarossa was a nightmare for Mediterranean maritime trade and threatened the safety of the coasts of the empire, so Charles gathered a huge force of Spanish, Portuguese, Italian and German troops, with 300 ships and 26,000 soldiers. The great victory achieved by this armada wasn't enough to put a stop to Barbarossa's excesses, however.

The original Madrid tapestry

The original tapestry of the *Review of the Troops at Barcelona*, which served as a model for this ceramic panel, is the second in a series entitled *The Conquest of Tunis by the Emperor Charles V*. This work, by Willem de Pannemaker, the great Flemish Renaissance tapestry master, is held in Madrid's Palacio Real (Royal Palace) and is part of a series of 12 tapestries of which only 10 have survived. In the 1730s, very high-quality copies were made in silk and wool, of which six can be viewed today in the tapestry room of Seville's Real Alcázar (Royal Alcázar).

LA CANINA

Death and the Cross

Church of San Gregorio
Calle Alfonso XII, 14
On Easter Saturday, the procession leaves at 7pm and returns at 11pm
May be visited in the church during the week before Holy Week

Every Easter Saturday, the procession of the Santo Entierro (Holy Burial) Fraternity sets out from the church of San Gregorio, bearing a strange image that has surprised and shocked onlookers since the late 17th century: a pensive skeleton resting its forehead on its right hand and holding a scythe in its left, while sitting on a globe of the world, representing the triumph of the Cross over death. Next to it lies a defeated dragon with an apple in its jaws to symbolise sin. In the background is a bare Cross with steps leaning up against it from which hang two shrouds, one with the message *Mors mortem superavit* (Death defeated death). A real mixture of symbolism and Baroque theatricality.

Although its official title is *Triumph of the Holy Cross over Death*, this is popularly known as *La Canina*, used in Seville to refer to a skeleton, in all likelihood originating from the expression 'to be as hungry as a hound' when referring to people who are all skin and bones.

This sculptural composition is the work of Antonio Cardoso de Quirós and dates from 1691. Even before this time, however, there is evidence of temporary 'mystery' tableaux with similar features being erected every year ... even the great Seville artist Valdés Leal, who painted the *Jeroglíficos* (*Hieroglyphs*) in the Hospital de la Caridad, may have taken part. In 1829, in the wake of the disastrous French invasion, the work was restored by sculptor Juan de Astorga.

Traditionally, the procession included the so-called allegorical cortège, made up of a large number of boys and girls dressed as angels, archangels, sibyls and prophets, but this custom was abandoned in the second half of the 20th century, sparking a lively debate.

La Canina first took part in the Holy Week processions of 1693, provoking 'real terror' according to an anonymous extant manuscript – you only need picture this display of macabre Baroque imagery parading through the gloomy streets of 17th-century Seville. Nowadays, more than three centuries later, this neo-Gothic procession, carried on the shoulders of 24 fraternity members, continues to shock both devotees and the curious alike. Not to mention the chuckles it brings to the lips of unbelievers.

GIANT BAMBOO

A tropical forest

Patio of the palace of the Marquis de la Motilla
Calle Cuna, 3

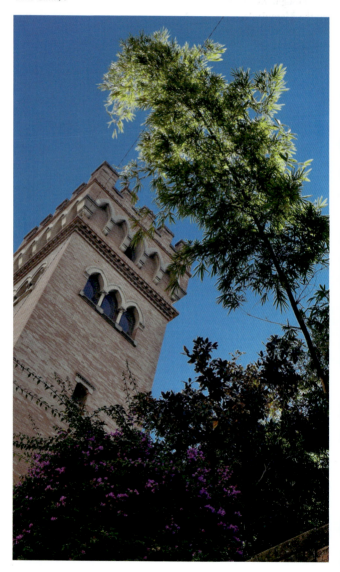

In the patio of the palace of the Marquis de la Motilla, on the corner of Calle Cuna and Calle Laraña, a group of enormous bamboo canes can be seen peeking over the walls and creating a sort of tropical forest in Seville's city centre. Known as a 'giant' or 'dragon' bamboo, the plant was brought to Seville following the round-the-world journey made by the Marquis de la Motilla, Miguel Desmaissieres, and his brother, Rafael. Both were particularly observant scholars and their travel diaries reveal that they noted down everything they saw and bought, especially in Japan. Their epic voyage lasted almost two years – from January 1886 to September 1887 – meaning that this incredible plant has been in the city for well over a century.

The plant's scientific name is *Dendrocalamus giganteus*, native to the tropical regions of Myanmar (Burma), Bhutan, China and Thailand and considered the tallest bamboo in the world – its canes reach 35 metres in height and measure almost 30 cm in diameter. It makes excellent building material and is used for all sorts of furniture and other objects, even ships' masts. The species' natural habitat is high tropical terrain at an altitude of up to 1,200 metres, so it needs the high humidity provided for it in the palace thanks to the micro-diffusers that water the canes.

Palace of the Marquis de la Motilla

Due to the expansion of the centre of Seville in the early 20th century, the Marquis de la Motilla commissioned modifications to his palace and the construction of new façades designed by the Italian architect Gino Coppedè in collaboration with Vicente Traver, who oversaw the technical side. The latter was a prominent architect in the Regionalist style, and also the man behind the Lope de Vega Theatre project and the Casino de la Exposición. The building works, which dragged on for a decade (1921–1931), clearly drew inspiration from Italian medieval architecture, reminiscent of Florence's Palazzo Vecchio. What is most remarkable is the great rectangular tower, stretching up 25 metres, with neo-Gothic arches in the windows. It stands guard over the patio, in the corner, where you can spot the giant bamboo peeking over.

PANTEÓN DE SEVILLANOS ILUSTRES

One of the most secret places in Seville

Facultad de Bellas Artes
Calle Laraña, 3
Friday 4.30pm–7.30pm
Admission free, advance booking not required
Guided tours by pupils from the Colegio Buen Pastor

 One of Seville's most secret places, the Pantheon of Illustrious Sevillians, lies hidden under the church of the Anunciación. Access to this crypt is via the patio of the Facultad de Bellas Artes (Faculty of Fine Arts), from where you go down a marble stairway that takes you to the north wall of the Epistle side. As you descend, you pass the old entrance from the church (a Renaissance work by the architect who designed the belfry of the Giralda, Hernán Ruiz II): this door has been shut since renovation works in the 20th century.

The crypt is wreathed in silence and enveloped in the metallic shimmer of its grey marble walls. It has the same layout as the church above: a Latin cross floor plan facing north, a central nave with no apse, and two small naves, one on each side, covered by vaults.

The pantheon commemorates major figures, both native and adopted, from Seville's long history. Worth highlighting among them is the prominent 16th-century humanist Benito Arias Montano, who was chaplain to Philip II and lived as a hermit in the Peña de Alájar (Huelva). Others buried here include figures as different as writer, historian and archaeologist José Gestoso and writer Cecilia Böhl de Faber (aka Fernán Caballero).

But if one tomb takes centre stage, it has to be that of Romantic writer Gustavo Adolfo Bécquer (see p. 246), who has been lying at rest here since 1913, alongside his brother Valeriano. His monument – the work of Eduardo Muñoz – has an angel carrying a copy of his famous work *Rimas* (Rhymes) in its left hand, with its feet on a pedestal adorned with scrollwork, where visitors leave scraps of paper with petitions (to pass an exam, to find true love ...) or even their favourite verses.

Built in 1579, the church of the Anunciación was part of the old Casa Profesa (Professed House) of the Society of Jesus until, following the expulsion of the Jesuits by a decree issued by Charles III, it became the seat of a university in 1771. In fact, the faculty's main patio still has the original marble pillars from the Casa's cloisters. During the 19th century, large numbers of tombs and pantheons (many from convents that had suffered under the French occupation) were installed in the old church and crypt – not until 1972 was substantial restoration work undertaken.

MUMMY OF MARÍA CORONEL

The king and the nun

Convent of Santa Inés
Doña María Coronel, 5
954 22 31 45
Tomb only open to the public on 2 December
Sweetmeats made in the convent are on sale: 9am–1pm & 4pm–6pm

Every 2 December, and for one day only, Seville's devotees of Doña María Coronel make their way to the Santa Inés convent, where her mummified body is on display in the church's lower choir, inside a glass case. This is one of the city's most important myths, somewhere between history and legend, the religious and the secular.

María was the oldest daughter of Alfonso Fernández Coronel, a prominent Castilian nobleman who was the *alguacil mayor* (chief bailiff) of the city of Seville. Born in the first half of the 14th century, the still very young María married Juan de la Cerda, grandson of Guzmán el Bueno and a direct descendant of Ferdinand III.

María's father and husband both chose to align themselves with Henry of Trastámara in the fight for the throne against his half-brother (and mortal enemy), King Peter I of Castile. In 1353 her father was captured and imprisoned on a charge of treason in the castle of Aguilar de la Frontera (Córdoba): he was condemned to be beheaded and his corpse burned in front of his four children, including María Coronel. In 1357 her husband was also imprisoned and then executed, and all his goods were confiscated. Having nowhere else to turn, María decided to enter the convent of Santa Clara, where her younger sister Aldonza had already sought refuge.

At this point legend clouds the picture. According to Sevillian myth, King Peter, who was smitten by the young widow, showed up at the convent begging for her favours. To avoid the monarch's unwanted attentions, she threw boiling oil over her face and hands in the convent kitchens. In the portrait hanging over the grille, the painter Valeriano Bécquer depicted these burns, which many visitors claim they can still see in the mummy.

Returning to the history books: it wasn't until Peter I died that María was able to recover her father's assets, and in 1374 she founded the convent of Santa Inés in the family palace. She remained in the convent until her death, which is believed to have taken place on 2 December 1411, when she was 77. Her remains were laid to rest next to those of her husband and a daughter – when they were moved at the end of the 17th century, the nuns were astonished to find that only María's body was still intact.

The church has one of Seville's oldest organs, which inspired Gustavo Adolfo Bécquer's story, *Maese Pérez el organista* (Master Pérez the Organist).

EMBALMED BODY OF ST ANGELA OF THE CROSS

Prayers for a saint, present in body

Convent of Santa Ángela de la Cruz
Calle Santa Ángela de la Cruz, 4
Daily 10am–1pm & 4pm–6.30pm

Although popular religious fervour is one of Seville's characteristics, the veneration for St Angela of the Cross (in the convent bearing her name) is clearly genuine. There are few places where, on any day of the week, you can get so close to the embalmed body of a saint for whom you can leave written petitions.

After going through the main entrance to the convent and being welcomed by the nun at the door, you head down a hallway to the right leading to a small and unprepossessing chapel.

Resting in a glass case in front of the altar is the embalmed body of the saint, preserved with a patina of wax on her face and hands. There is an urn on a side table for the faithful to leave their written petitions to 'Mother Angelita', as she was popularly known – requests for help in finding work, or a husband or wife, or to ask for the healing of a sick relative, and so on.

A statue of Our Lady of Health, which comes from the church of Santa Lucía in which Angelita was christened, looks down over the Baroque altar.

Accompanying the saint on one side of the chapel lies the body of Sor María Purísima, her successor for over 50 years, herself canonised by Pope Francis in 2015.

In 1875 Ángela Guerrero (1846–1933) founded the religious order, Hermanas de la Compañía de la Cruz (Sisters of the Company of the Cross) in Seville, an institution devoted to social work. She was dearly loved throughout Andalusia, particularly for her dedication to the poor and infirm. When she died on 2 March 1932, tributes poured in from people of all backgrounds and creeds. Two days later, the Republican City Council unanimously decided to rename Calle Alcázares (where the order's headquarters are located) in her honour.

A convent open every 2 March

The inner patios may only be visited on 2 March (the anniversary of St Angela's death) and during Easter week, when the nuns decorate them to mark the Resurrection of Christ. On these days you can also visit the room she lived in, where souvenirs of her life have been preserved.

The building currently houses an old peoples' home as well as a boarding school for girls, both run by the Sisters of the Cross.

SCALLOP SHELL

The start of street-numbering in Seville

Calle José Gestoso, 1

A large stone shell nailed to the wall of a house at the beginning of Calle José Gestoso barely merits a glance as passers-by walk down this busy Seville shopping street just behind Plaza de la Encarnación.

According to records going back to 1384, this thoroughfare was nicknamed '*Venera*', or 'scallop shell' street, as early as the 14th century. But what is really unusual about this great shell is that, as agreed by the City Council in 1845 – and still today – it marks the start of the numbering of Seville's streets within the city walls, with No. 1 on each street being allocated to the building closest to the shell.

The scallop shell is not known to have any other function than as a point of reference – whether it was simply a decorative feature or if it indicated that the house or street had some other specific use. A popular commercial thoroughfare throughout the ages, possibly from before the conquest of Seville by Ferdinand III of Castile in the 13th century, the street lost its original name in 1918, taking that of José Gestoso, a local historian, archaeologist and writer who had died a few months earlier, in September 1917, and was born at No. 5 on that very street. Gestoso was a tireless defender of the city's historical heritage and had been involved in the restoration of the Giralda, the Torre del Oro and the Alcázar. He himself would almost certainly not have agreed with changing the name of one of the city's most symbolic streets, known for centuries as *Venera*.

Venus, Viernes *and the Way of St James*

The *venera* is the shell of a bivalve mollusc known as the scallop, whose scientific name is *Pecten jacobaeus*. The scallop shell in the Calle José Gestoso displays the concave side of its wider valve and only has 10 grooves, whereas the real shell has 14. Its scientific name refers to its use as a badge of honour for pilgrims on the Way of St James (Camino de Santiago), which is also why it is known as the 'pilgrim's shell'. Long before the opening up of that pilgrim route, the scallop shell was associated with Venus, the Roman goddess of love (which is where it gets its name) as well as *viernes* (Spanish for Friday), the day on which the goddess was worshipped. The *venera* was also widely used by the Hispano-Visigoths and the Muslims, for whom it had great mystical significance.

NEARBY
Peacock tile
Calle José Gestoso, 3

The large ceramic tile (*azulejo*) at No. 3, bearing the inscription *El pavo real* (The Peacock), was originally to be found on the façade of an old inn of the same name, which disappeared in the 1970s.

RELIEFS IN THE CAPILLA DE LOS LUISES

Fantastical images symbolising the degradation of man through sin

Capilla de los Luises
Calle Trajano, 35

The most surprising and unusual thing about the Capilla de los Luises (De los Luises chapel) – an Italianate neo-Gothic edifice built by Seville architect Aníbal González between 1916 and 1920 – is to be found on its façade, in the complex array of iconography carved at eye level into the red brick, catching distracted passers-by unawares.

To the left of the chapel's main entrance is a decorative frieze of phytomorphic motifs, interlaced with religious and fantastical images:

relief work such as a lizard that has been worn away and lost its head because of the superstitious caresses of passers-by; an ogre with a sword, looking defiantly out at us; a terrible dragon; a dog that threatens onlookers, its jaws wide open; a bearded man hitting a skull with a stick ... Bestial and monstrous images embodying Evil and the multiple forms of man's degradation through sin, and somewhat reminiscent of the iconography of Romanesque sculpture.

In the central section, other ornamental figures show symbols from Christ's Passion: a cock puffing out its chest, representing Peter who denied Jesus three times; Christ bearing the Cross; three angels; the veil of Veronica; and the Instruments of the Passion (among them, a hammer and three nails, the spear and the sponge, and the ladders).

Symbols of the four Evangelists

To the left of the entrance are three windows flanked by four pilasters. Each is dedicated to one of the four Evangelists, with his symbol at the bottom and a little statue towards the top. This tetramorphic depiction starts on the left, with the figure of an angel, followed by an ox, an eagle and a lion. As is well known, these delicate brick carvings refer to the four Evangelists: Matthew, Luke, John and Mark (in that order).

According to the Old Testament, one of the prophet Ezekiel's visions (possibly influenced by Babylonian astrology and the symbolism of ancient Egypt) featured four creatures with human faces at the front and animal faces at the back. It was St Jerome at the end of the 4th century who associated these four figures with the Evangelists, a tradition that lived on in medieval sculpture and painting.

The Tarot card representing the world also features the four symbols of the Evangelists. In the heavens, the eagle reflects the power of the intellect and the word, and the angel stands for feelings and love. And below, on Earth, the lion represents creativity or sexual activity whereas the ox leads us towards the material realm.

MARKER OF THE FLOOD OF 1961 ⑬

A reminder of the historic bursting of the banks of the Guadalquivir

Corner of Calle Santa Ana and the Alameda de Hércules

ALAS 9 DE LA NOCHE DEL MIERC.
28 DE DIC.° DE 1796 SIENDO ASIS-
TENTE DE ESTA CIVDAD EL EXMO. S.
D. MANVEL CANDIDO MORENO SV-
BIÓ EL RIO EN LOS CONTORNOS EX-
DIORES DE ELLA HASTA EL NIVEL COR-
RESP.° AL PIÉ DE ESTE AZVLEJO.

A ESTE NIVEL
LLEGARON LAS
AGUAS EN LA
INUNDACION DE
SEVILLA EN
EL 1961

On the corner of the Alameda and Calle Santa Ana, two commemorative tiles act as reminders of two great floods. The first, which stands at a considerable height (some 3 metres), marks where the waters reached at midnight on Wednesday 28 December 1796. The second marks the flood of 1961.

When the Arabs named the city's river *al-wādi al-kabīr*, they knew what they were doing. The 'big river' has given the city everything: its main source of communications; the basis for its economic activities; and its fertile agricultural lands. But it has also been the source of serious problems, such as the floods that periodically lay waste to the city. These terrible flash floods are due to the irregular volume of water carried by the Guadalquivir and its tributaries, the Tagarete and Tamarguillo streams and the Guadaíra river, alternating harsh droughts with bouts of heavy rainfall.

One of the places most affected by this phenomenon was the Alameda de Hércules. It was no coincidence that there was a lagoon here in ancient times, the result of a meander in the original course of the river.

The bursting of the banks of the Tamarguillo on 25 November 1961 was the last time the city fell victim to flooding, and the worst case in its recent history. Almost three-quarters of the area was flooded; the volume of water reached some 4 million cubic metres, destroying everything in its path and affecting a quarter of the city's population, which stood just shy of 500,000 at the time – over 30,000 people lost their homes.

The northern part of the city, around the Alameda, had a large number of working-class rented dwellings: the communal tenements known as *corrales de vecinos* (see p. 112). The heart of working-class Seville was flooded for three days: the water reached a height of 1.8 metres, turning the area into an impromptu lake that could only be navigated by rowing boats. Many of the thousands of families who were cut off without supplies took refuge on their terraces and rooftops while they waited for help. Seville was declared a disaster zone and an aid caravan called Operación Clavel (Operation Carnation) was sent from Madrid. It ended in tragedy due to an accident involving the light aircraft accompanying it, causing the deaths of 20 people and leaving dozens more seriously injured.

The flood signalled the end for the Alameda's *corrales de vecinos*, which were already in a terrible state of disrepair. Many of the residents were forced to abandon the historic centre and move to social housing estates in the suburbs, changing the urban landscape of this area.

HOMBRE DE PIEDRA

A marble torso that gave its name to a street

Calle Hombre de Piedra, 10

I n the San Lorenzo district, towards the back of Casa de las Sirenas (House of the Mermaids), there is a narrow street with the odd name of Hombre de Piedra (Stone Man). At its beginning, on the right-hand pavement and at ground level, you can see a little niche with the marble statue of a largely disfigured human form that gave the street its name, stretching back to the 18th century and possibly earlier.

There are numerous theories regarding the origin of this Roman torso, where you can still make out a toga wrapped around the body. The most widely accepted holds that the statue comes from some local thermal baths, which were still in use during the Islamic era under the name of Baños de la Estatua (Baths of the Statue). Another hypothesis is that the statue comes from a Roman pleasure villa.

The fact is that over the centuries this marble torso probably ended up as what Seville locals call a *botarruedas* – architectural features like columns and millstones inserted into the lower sections of walls to protect the façades from the wheels of passing carriages.

An old legend gives a different version, however, and a terrible one at that. The story has it that a man called Matías el Rubio refused to kneel as a cortège bearing the holy sacraments to perform the last rites passed by. No laughing matter, given that an old law stipulated that people must '*kneel down under pain of a fine and loss of their mount and, in the case of a Moor aged more than 14, the loss of their clothing*' ... as can be seen from a stone plaque dating from 1714 in the church of San Salvador. In this case, our man not only lost his clothes, but was struck by lightning and turned to stone for blasphemy, leaving the 'stone man' seen today.

NEARBY
Final headquarters of the Spanish Inquisition

The block to the left, on Calle Jesús del Gran Poder, housed the Jesuit college known as the Becas Coloradas (Red Hoods). In 1785 it became the final headquarters of the Spanish Inquisition, as a huge flood had forced the permanent evacuation of the castle of San Jorge in Triana (see p. 206). In 1810, when the Holy Office was abolished during the French occupation, the Inquisitors fled to Ceuta. They returned to their Seville headquarters when the Inquisition was restored by Ferdinand VII and stayed there until it was abolished in 1834.

SPHINXES AT CASA DE LAS SIRENAS

The enigma of the Recreo de la Alameda

Centro Cívico Las Sirenas
Alameda de Hércules, 30
Monday–Saturday 9am–9pm
Admission free

Due to its noble appearance and Gallic style, the palatial residence at No. 30 on the Alameda de Hércules has been surprising visitors to this working-class neighbourhood since the mid-19th century. At the entrance, you are met by two bronze sphinxes, thought to have been cast in Paris. The unknown origin and function of these two mythological creatures led to their being confused with mermaids, so the building became popularly known as Casa de las Sirenas (House of the Mermaids).

Two larger sphinxes, which have since disappeared, used to adorn the start of the double ramp for carriages arriving at the residence. They may have ended up at the home of an antique dealer.

The sphinxes here are shown in accordance with Greek mythology – they have a woman's face, a lion's body and the wings of a bird. In mythology, the sphinx learnt the art of formulating riddles from the muses and it strangled people who were unable to solve them. In ancient Egypt, they were placed at the entrance to temples to indicate that the secrets were protected from the uninitiated.

Masonic architecture often used the image of the sphinx, which might be one explanation for the use of these figures in the building.

Identical railings to those in London's Kensington Gardens

The building's classical style marks it out from the other houses in the neighbourhood. It has four identical façades surrounded by a garden bordered by an attractive railing ... curiously enough, identical to one in London's Kensington Gardens.

Built in 1864, the Recreo (Pleasure House) de la Alameda was the work of Joaquín Fernández Ayarragaray, an architect from the Basque region of Guipúzcoa, who was a professor at Seville's School of Fine Arts. Apparently, it was commissioned by Lázaro Fernández de Angulo, often erroneously referred to as the Marquis de Esquivel, who wanted to build a residence in the style of Madrid's upper classes. At that time, Seville had come under the influence of the *corte chica* (little court), presided over by the Duke and Duchess of Montpensier, and building styles were influenced by those of Paris.

The original owner only lived in the house for six years, and it then passed from one owner to another until finally vacated in 1971, inhabited by cats and haunted by ghosts. In 1992 it was purchased by the City Council to be renovated and used as a civic centre.

STATUE OF FERDINAND VII

The travelling sculpture

Espacio Santa Clara
Calle Becas (no number)
icas.sevilla.org/espacios/espacio-santa-clara
Daily 10am–8pm
Admission free

I n a corner of the gardens of the old convent of Santa Clara, opposite the tower of Don Fadrique, a statue of Ferdinand VII of Bourbon, one of the most reviled kings in Spanish history, is to be found quite literally hiding. This huge bronze shows the king in military uniform, with an ermine cape and a crown of laurels (but without the hands and sword lost during the statue's final journey).

After the French troops invaded in 1808, Napoleon forced Ferdinand VII and his father, Charles IV, to abdicate in his favour, with the ultimate aim of placing his brother Joseph Bonaparte on the throne. This act triggered the Peninsular War. When that ended in 1814, Ferdinand returned, becoming an absolute monarch: he reneged on the constitution signed by the Courts of Cádiz (to which he had sworn) and reinstated the Spanish Inquisition.

One of his most loyal followers was a sinister and bizarre character called Charles d'Espagnac (Carlos de España), who despite hailing from France had fought on the Spanish side. The king named him Grandee of Spain and General Captain of Catalonia, and during the five years he served he was responsible for all sorts of excesses, killing anyone suspected of being a liberal. It was during this period that de España commissioned the bronze statue from French sculptor Pierre Joseph Chardigny, to be erected in the main square of the Palau de Barcelona in 1831.

But it wasn't there long – in 1840 Maria Christina, the widow (and niece) of the king, took it with her into exile to adorn the gardens of the Château de Malmaison in Paris. Here it remained until her daughter, the Infanta María Luisa Fernanda and her husband, Antoine d'Orléans, son of the king of France, fled following the declaration of the French Second Republic. Shortly afterwards, Napoleon III sent the statue to the palace of San Telmo in Seville (see p. 236), which would become its new home.

When she was widowed, the daughter of Ferdinand VII donated some of the palace gardens to the city of Seville, where María Luisa park was later built. The statue moved back and forth between various parts of this verdant space until, with the declaration of the Second Spanish Republic in 1931, it was taken to its present location, along with other pieces belonging to Seville's Museo Arqueológico (Archaeological Museum).

On the way, the statue lost its sword and hands, which apparently ended up being sold at the Thursday street market on Calle Feria.

TORRE DE DON FADRIQUE

Legends surrounding the haunted tower

Convent of Santa Clara
Calle Becas (no number)
icas.sevilla.org/espacios/espacio-santa-clara
Daily 10am–8pm
Admission free

An inconspicuous door on the right-hand side of the patio of the old convent of Santa Clara leads to the gardens, where a proud and solitary 30-metre-high medieval tower hides away in a little-known spot.

Over the years, all sorts of theories have sprung up regarding this *torre encantada* (haunted tower), as it is popularly known. What is certain is who it was built for. Over the doorway of this unique example of secular Gothic architecture is a Latin inscription recording that the Infante Don Fadrique, the second son of Ferdinand III, King of Castile, and his first wife, Queen Elizabeth of Swabia, ordered it be built in 1252.

When he was just 15, the Infante was sent to Germany, to the court of Frederick II, the Holy Roman Emperor, with the intention of staking a claim to the inheritance of his mother, who had died five years earlier. Later, in 1245, Fadrique and his brothers were called upon by their father to help in the siege of Jaén. He subsequently took part in the conquest of Seville, for which he was granted numerous properties in the resulting share-out of the city.

One of these gifts was a group of Almohad buildings in today's San Lorenzo district, where he ordered this tower to be built, and where a century later the Clarist Franciscan convent would be built. In fact, Fadrique did not get to live here long, as he was exiled in 1260, accused of treason by his elder brother, Alfonso X, who a few years later sentenced him to death by drowning.

Notable among the tower's many legends is the one about the supposed love affair within its walls between Fadrique and his French stepmother, Queen Joan of Ponthieu, the beautiful young widow of his father, Ferdinand III. This relationship scandalised both court and commoners, so Joan was forced to leave for France and Alfonso X ordered his brother's death. However, this legend clearly has no basis in fact, given that Queen Joan returned to France in 1252, the year her husband died, and the very year that work began on the tower.

From 1925 to 1946, these secluded historic gardens served as the municipal archaeological museum. Some of the pieces belonging to the collection still stand in the shade of an enormous laurel tree, probably the oldest in Seville, and a gigantic Swiss cheese plant (*Monstera deliciosa*).

TORRE DE LOS PERDIGONES

The last vestiges of the San Francisco de Paula foundry

Calle Resolana, 42
Tuesday–Sunday noon–5pm

Standing 45 metres high, the Torre de los Perdigones (Gunshot Tower) dwarfs the surrounding buildings in the working-class districts in the north of the city. This square brick tower is all that remains of what was once the San Francisco de Paula foundry, commonly known as the 'gunshot factory'. It was one of the city's many foundries, which from 1890 manufactured lead plates and bars, water pipes, parts for ovens, zinc bathtubs and so on.

The Macarena district (the old suburb outside the city walls) and the northern part of the old town (particularly the San Gil and San Julián districts) underwent major industrialisation from the late 19th century until the 1950s, thanks to good nearby land and rail connections, available land and a willing workforce.

The tower's name comes from the fact that the factory produced sizeable quantities of gunshot pellets, the little lead balls that filled the ammunition cartridges used in the popular sport of hunting. A normal cartridge would contain between 200 and 300 pellets.

The manufacturing method used was patented by Welshman Charles Watts in 1782. Once the lead plates had been raised to the top of the tower via a system of pulleys, they were melted in a furnace. The molten material was then poured through sieves with holes of different sizes, which determined the different calibres of the pellets. The drops of lead fell freely down inside, making perfect spherical shapes thanks to the height of the tower. They then dropped into a tank of water, where they cooled and solidified, before finally rolling down a ramp to the outside.

There is another gunshot tower in the centre of Brussels: see *Secret Brussels*, from the same publisher.

Camera obscura

In 2007 a camera obscura was opened at the top of the tower. This is one of only a few in Europe – the oldest is in Edinburgh and dates from 1835. Thanks to this optical instrument, which has a series of magnification lenses and reflective mirrors, a moving image of the city can be projected onto a white screen in a closed, darkened room. Visitors are surprised to see a 'live' view of the Macarena district and its walls, the Alameda de Hércules or the Isla de la Cartuja.

MODERNIST ELECTRICAL SUBSTATION

Lamplighters and electricians

Calle Feria, 154

Although currently in residential use, the building at No. 154 Calle Feria – one of the few modernist buildings in the city – was once an industrial facility. In 1905 the Compañía Sevillana de Electricidad (Seville Electricity Company) commissioned the great Seville architect Aníbal González to design this electrical substation to store and supply energy. Its façade reflects the typical modernist interest in decoration and use of organic forms. Highlights include the tiled signage, the railings on the main balcony, the mouldings of the arches and the ornamental balustrade at the top.

Modernism became a widespread trend throughout central Europe at the turn of the 19th and 20th centuries, finally reaching Spain, where it enjoyed a cautious reception in Seville – it was too innovative an artistic language for a city rooted in tradition. In fact, this is one of the few buildings in the style developed by the young Aníbal González, just three years after completing his training. One year before, in 1904, he had designed an enormous electricity plant for the same company on Avenida de la Borbolla, a piece of industrial heritage that has sadly been lost.

At the dawn of the 20th century, a war was raging for control of the local energy market. The Sociedad Catalana para el Alumbrado por Gas (Catalan Gas Lighting Company), known simply as La Catalana, had controlled public lighting since 1866. Its rival, the Compañía Sevillana de Electricidad, founded in 1894, was supplying electric lighting, a cleaner, more modern and more efficient technology. The fierce rivalry between the two companies often spilled over into the workplace, with frequent fights breaking out between lamplighters and electricians – a lamplighter even died in one of them.

Within the context of this struggle, a number of commissions for the design and construction of electrical substations and factories were awarded to Seville's most prominent architects. In 1912 the Compañia Catalana de Gas y Electricidad (Catalan Gas and Electricity Company) commissioned Aníbal González to design its most iconic building, the gas and electricity factory in the Porvenir district, now converted into a sports centre.

NEARBY
Substations in neo-Mudéjar style
San Luis, 118
González Cuadrado, 47
Scattered across the historic centre are a number of little buildings in neo-Mudéjar style; their windows have ironwork arches and translucent coloured glass. These are the electrical substations built by architect Antonio Arévalo from 1911 onwards for the Catalana de Gas, of which two are located in this very neighbourhood.

MUDÉJAR WINDOW IN OMNIUM SANCTORUM

A delicate work of 14th-century craftsmanship

Calle Feria, 98
Monday–Friday 10am–1pm & 7.30pm–9pm

One could be forgiven for not noticing the beautiful ogival window in the main façade of the church of Omnium Sanctorum, above the entrance leading to Calle Feria. This delicate work was executed by master builders, using reddish bricks and tiles that were cut (using the *alicatado* technique) into little white, black, turquoise and honey-yellow pieces to make star-shaped mosaics.

The window dates to around the mid-14th century during the reign of Peter I, when the pre-existing church (severely damaged in the 1356 earthquake) was rebuilt. That church, known as Omnium Sanctorum (All Saints), had apparently incorporated the remains of a pre-existing Almohad mosque.

The epicentre of the terrible earthquake (magnitude 8.0) of 24 August 1356 was in Cape St Vincent (Portugal), but it caused widespread damage to many of Seville's buildings of Islamic origin. The worst was the fall of the Great Mosque's *yamur* – the four enormous bronze balls that crowned the tower of the minaret (today's Giralda).

Twelve heads

The church's main façade, in Calle Feria, has a curious piece of relief work featuring 12 human heads (the 12 Apostles?) on the magnificent, pointed 13th-century entrance arch, carved in stone with archivolts.

Uprising of the Green Pendant

The church's baptistery was originally the funeral chapel of the Cervantes family, who (as may be seen from the top of the 17th-century grille) were '*Caballeros Veinticuatro*' (literally, Twenty-four Gentlemen) of Seville – something like town councillors – who belonged to the upper echelons of society.

The chapel housed the *Pendón Verde* (Green Pendant), a standard taken from the Almohad forces in battle and raised in the famous riots which broke out on 8 May 1521. On that day, the residents of the Feria district, who were starving, rose up against the authorities. After a lengthy struggle, the leaders were executed and their severed heads hung from the window of the nearby palace of the Marquises de la Algaba (see p. 46).

CENTRO DEL MUDÉJAR

One of the city's least-known and most unusual interpretation centres

Plaza Calderón de la Barca (no number)
955 47 25 25
Monday–Friday 10am–2pm & 5pm–8pm, Saturday 10am–2pm
Admission free

In the square behind Omnium Sanctorum and the Feria market stands the palace of the Marquises de la Algaba. This building now houses one of the city's least-known and most unusual interpretation centres: the Centro del Mudéjar (Mudéjar Centre). Opened in 2013, the exhibition rooms take you on a thrilling journey through Mudéjar art. Among the 111 pieces on display, particular highlights are a baptismal font, stamps, jars, tiles, plasterwork and Gothic headstones. The most secret and interesting piece in the palace is the fabulous polychrome Renaissance wooden ceiling in the room known as the Salón de Doña Leonor, whose design combines plant motifs and coats of arms. By a miracle, it is in very good condition, having lain hidden under a false ceiling.

The centre's beautiful entrance is the foremost piece of secular Mudéjar architecture of its kind in Seville, second only to the one at the palace of Peter I in the Real Alcázar (Royal Alcázar). Its window is decorated with multifoil arches and mosaics made from broken pieces of blue, green, white and ochre tiles (*alicatado* technique). In the building's frieze, you can see the gap that would have housed the Guzmán coat of arms, now missing. Also of note is the two-storey defensive tower built entirely of brick.

Formerly there was a little arch and a raised walkway connecting the palace directly with the church, but this was demolished in the 19th century. The central patio, which still has a number of marble columns from Genoa, is an oasis of tranquillity amidst the hubbub of the surrounding neighbourhood.

The palace was built in the mid-15th century by the first lord of La Algaba, Juan de Guzmán, in an area that was a major commercial hub for food and agriculture and where the Feria market currently stands. The building has undergone many vicissitudes over the centuries, particularly in the 19th century, when it became a theatre, a tenement block, a summer cinema ... until, in 2002, it re-emerged like a phoenix from the ruins following renovations undertaken with EU funding.

Mudéjars: Muslims in Christian lands

The Mudéjars were Muslims who were allowed to continue living in the lands conquered by the Christians. They were often excellent artisans and builders and were responsible for this mix of Castilian Gothic and Almohad art, so common in Seville.

CHARCOAL YARD
ON CALLE PARRAS

A reminder of the warmth of yesteryear

Calle Parras, 2
carboneriaparras.com
Monday–Saturday 9am–3pm

A stone's throw from the Puerta de la Macarena there is a family business selling charcoal, the last one remaining in the city. Crossing its threshold takes you back in time, surrounded by the charcoal and soot-blackened walls and floors. Hanging from the walls are esparto-grass baskets, used by the present owner's grandfather to gather the charcoal and bring it back by donkey from the old train station in Plaza de Armas.

Here you can find holm-oak charcoal from Extremadura; tiny particles of coal dust; small pieces of *cisco picón* (charcoal from the smaller branches of the tree, used for braziers to which a sprig of dried lavender was added to give a pleasant smell); mineral residues (anthracite and coke); wood for fuel; and also, as a concession to modernity, butane gas.

The yard was founded by Francisco Aguilar over a hundred years ago, in the early 20th century. As he already owned another yard on Calle Cruz Verde, he purchased an old flour mill to store the charcoal before distributing it to the various depots throughout the district. In the 1950s his son Manuel built this yard on the site of the old mill, where it still stands today, thanks to the work of Luis, now the third generation. As well as the Aguilar family, numerous workers have passed through its doors, especially between the 1940s and 1960s.

Seville's charcoal yards

Until electricity and gas became widespread, charcoal yards provided a key service in towns and villages. Charcoal was essential for cooking, in the ever-popular *cocinas económicas* ('economic stoves') and for lighting braziers to heat the home. As such, there was a charcoal yard on almost every square and street in Seville, where it was difficult to tell the men apart from the women, so charcoal-smudged were their skin and hair. People not fortunate enough to have their own premises became travelling salesmen, hauling great sacks of charcoal through the streets. The luckier ones might have a mule to help with this, every bit as tired and blackened as its owner. An arduous way of making a living ...

SOLOMONIC SYMBOLS IN THE CHURCH OF SAN LUIS DE LOS FRANCESES

The temple that heralds the Heavenly Jerusalem

Calle San Luis, 37
954 55 02 07
Tuesday–Sunday 10am–2pm & 4pm–8pm
For group tours: sanluis_visitas@dipusevilla.es

San Luis de los Franceses – the masterpiece of architect Leonardo de Figueroa – is the most magnificent Baroque church in Seville. Built between 1699 and 1731 for the novitiate of the Society of Jesus (Jesuits), the church (currently deconsecrated) hides a number of secrets from the uninitiated. The most striking is that it was designed as a temple of Solomon, the 'perfect' temple, the place of divine wisdom, conceived of as a complex series of symbols heralding the Heavenly or New Jerusalem, the city of God.

Its floor plan consists of a large circle inside a Greek cross whose arms point to the four cardinal points in reference to the imagined plan of the temple of the Israelites. Although Renaissance and Baroque scholars thought that the Old Testament temple had a rectangular floor plan, the Jesuit Order went back to the medieval idea that linked it to the Dome of the Rock and the basilica of the Holy Sepulchre in Jerusalem, both of which had circular floor plans.

Sixteen pillars rise up towards the dome, flanking niches and chapels. These pillars – known as Solomonic or barley-sugar columns due to their corkscrew, helicoidal appearance – are a representation of the two pillars, Boaz and Jachin, which stood on either side of the entrance to the temple in Jerusalem, symbolising strength and stability. Another two Solomonic engaged columns feature prominently in the upper level of the façade.

The Solomonic symbols are seen most clearly in the impressive dome. Here the frescoes by Lucas Valdés faithfully include all the elements of the temple. In the central recess and behind the allegorical figure representing Religion is the *Ark of the Covenant*, the central element of the Holy of Holies (the most sacred part of the temple), the details of whose construction God explained to Moses (Exodus: 25–31). The Ark is protected by a gold lid known as the *propitiatory* (mercy seat), with two gold cherubim facing each other, their wings unfurled.

Further to the right are depictions of the *Menorah* (the great golden seven-branched oil candlestick), the *Brazen Altar*, the *Veil* that closed off the Holy of Holies, the *Molten Sea*, the *Altar of Burnt Offering*, where animals were sacrificed in God's honour, the *Table of Showbread* (with its twelve unleavened loaves in two columns of six) and the *Altar of Incense*, which even features the smoke of burning incense.

ORATORY OF THE PUERTA DE CÓRDOBA

The legend of a martyr

Puerta de Córdoba
Church of San Hermenegildo – Calle Puerta de Córdoba, 1
954 37 17 90
Church open: Thursday 7.30pm; bank holidays & Sunday 1pm
Visits by prior appointment:
hermandaddesanhermenegildodesevilla@hotmail.com

To visit this enigmatic oratory dedicated to the Visigoth King Hermenegild, in the heart of the Puerta de Córdoba, you need to book in advance. The oratory is accessed through a door in the church, which dates from 1616. After crossing the patio of the tower/gateway and climbing a narrow stairway, you'll see the stone altar of a little chapel covered by a magnificent 16th-century Mudéjar vaulted ceiling.

One of Seville's most popular legends is based on the belief that Hermenegild was imprisoned and martyred here on the orders of his father, Leovigild, in the 6th century. A stone plaque on the wall bears witness to the story: '*Oh, you, whoever pass by, pay veneration at this place consecrated with the Holy Blood of King Hermenegild.*'

In fact, the martyrdom could never have taken place here as this is a medieval gateway, built around the 12th century, many years after the event. The legend is founded on the erroneous belief, held until the 19th century, that the Seville city wall dates back to Roman times and was built by Julius Caesar, although it is in fact of Islamic origin. This myth has undoubtedly saved the tower from demolition.

The Puerta de Córdoba is one of the three gateways still standing today (see p. 56). This is the most interesting of the three, and also the least well known, joined to the Puerta de la Macarena by the longest surviving stretch of wall. It consists of a tower/gateway sticking out of the wall, with an l-shaped entrance leading to an open patio. This type of military construction was extremely useful in a siege: from there it was possible to beat back assailants by throwing boiling oil over them or sending down a volley of arrows.

Hermenegild, the martyr king

In 579 the Visigoth King Leovigild appointed his son Hermenegild governor of Baetica, whose capital was Seville. Although Arianism was the official religion, Hermenegild was married to a Frankish princess who, with the help of Bishop San Leandro, succeeded in converting him to Catholicism. Leovigild demanded that his son return to the Arian faith and immediately attend the court in Toledo. A war broke out between father and son that would lead to the siege of Seville. After his defeat, Hermenegild was captured in Córdoba and subsequently taken to Tarragona to be executed. That's why he is depicted in shackles and with an axe smiting his head.

CENTRO DE DOCUMENTACIÓN DE LAS ARTES ESCÉNICAS

A magic library

Santa Lucía, 10
955 92 88 50
juntadeandalucia.es/cultura/redportales/cdaea
Guided tours (must be booked in advance): the first Monday (11am) and Thursday (4pm) of each month

Since 2012, the beautiful and magnificently renovated nave of the old Gothic church of Santa Lucía has been home to the Documentation Centre for the Performing Arts, an institution that entered into an agreement with the Magic Circle of Seville (the association representing the city's magicians) to house the Fondo de Ilusionismo de Andalusía (Andalusian Collection of Illusionary Magic). The collection includes a large number of books, magazines and video recordings that are key to understanding the history of magic not only in Seville but throughout Andalusia, as well as a major repertory of lecture notes – a fundamental resource when it comes to passing on magical knowledge, which is frequently ephemeral and shrouded in secrecy. The collection, which is continually expanding thanks to purchases and donations, is the third largest in Spain, after the Fundación March and the archives of the Biblioteca Nacional (Spain's National Library), and number one in terms of video recordings. The oldest and undoubtedly most important book is Jean Nicolas Ponsin's *Curso completo de prestidigitación o la hechicería antigua y moderna explicada* (*Complete Course in Conjuring or Old and Modern Sorcery Explained*) dating from around 1880 and published in Valencia by the Pascual Aguilar bookshop. Pablo Minguet (1733–78) was the first Spanish author of books on illusionary magic, with works including *Juegos de manos o sea arte de hacer diabluras* (*Sleight of Hand Tricks or the Art of Doing Devilry*). The origins of the collection go back to a time when the city's magicians, who used to meet

in the back room of a bar on the Alameda de Hércules, saw their library almost lost to flooding on one of the numerous occasions that the Guadalquivir burst its banks, laying waste to the city. The collection then had to be shared out among all the members of the Magic Circle for safe keeping.

Entranceway that moved

The original doorway to the church of Santa Lucía was removed and installed in the church of Santa Catalina in the 1930s. Santa Lucía was secularised by the City Council in 1868 and became the headquarters of the Tertulia Democrática, Reunión de Artesanos Honrados (Democratic Gathering, Meeting of Honourable Artisans). Over the years, it has served the most varied of functions, from match factory and cinema to garage and rehearsal room.

ISLAMIC WALL IN JARDINES DEL VALLE

(26)

The most secret section of Seville's medieval city wall

Jardines del Valle
Calle María Auxiliadora, 33
Daily 8am–10pm

One of the best-preserved and least-known sections of Seville's medieval wall is tucked away in the gardens known as the Jardines del Valle, a location recorded as early as the 15th century, when the convent of the same name was founded. Separating the gardens from the surrounding buildings are 300 metres of perimeter walls approximately 12 metres high and 2.45 metres wide, constructed using a mud-wall technique involving lime, clay, sand and stones. This stretch of wall also has two well-preserved turrets.

The medieval wall was built in the 12th century by the Almoravids. In the 13th century, the Almohads reinforced and extended it, with some sections being heightened by a further 2 metres.

The Roman wall had protected a much smaller city, centred around the cathedral area, Plaza de la Alfalfa and Plaza de la Encarnación. The enormous expansion during the Islamic era (by which time the enclosed area measured some 250 hectares) was mainly due to the new role of Isbiliya as the mainland capital of the Almohad empire. It also led to the construction of a floating or pontoon bridge, the supply of water via the Caños de Carmona (see p. 128) and the new Great Mosque. Over its entire length, the wall had 166 square and octagonal turrets with 50 metres of wall between each one.

The wall had a dozen gates and a number of secondary access points. The medieval gateways were Sol, Osario, Carmona, Carne, Jerez, Arenal, Triana, Real (the old Puerta de Goles), San Juan, Barqueta, Macarena and Córdoba – only the last two are still standing, as well as the Aceite entrance. The last gate to be demolished in Seville – the Puerta del Sol, in 1873 – was the closest to these gardens.

After Seville's conquest by King Ferdinand III in 1248, the city wall lost its original defensive function but was useful in tackling the city's old enemy: the river floods that periodically laid waste to it.

NEARBY
Wall of the Macarena

The original wall measured some 7 km. As well as this hidden stretch of it, you can also see the section that joined the Puerta de la Macarena with the tower/gateway of the Puerta de Córdoba (see p. 52), with its Torre Blanca (White Tower). Another section of wall has survived in Callejón del Agua, at the back of the Alcázar. It is estimated that some 70 per cent (around 5 km) of the old city wall still exists, hidden among the surrounding buildings.

LABORATORIO MUNICIPAL DE HIGIENE

27

A temple to science

Avenida María Auxiliadora, 16
955 47 33 43
laboratorio@sevilla.org
Visits by prior appointment, Thursday 10am–1pm

Opposite the Jardines del Valle, the Municipal Hygiene Laboratory, with a history stretching back over a hundred years, continues to be a major urban landmark, but this institution is as unknown as it is important to healthcare in Seville.

On its pale-yellow façade there is an array of surnames of illustrious figures associated with science and health: Pasteur, Koch, Roux, Berzelius, Ferrán, Jenner, Ramón y Cajal, Lavoisier, Curie and Bertholet. This is a roadside lesson in the history of science, particularly in times when epidemics spread like wildfire and vaccination was essential. Which is why pride of place is taken by the father of immunology, the English surgeon Edward Jenner, who discovered a crucial vaccine against smallpox, alongside Koch, the discoverer of the tuberculosis and cholera bacilli, and the great Pasteur, a key player in the development of antibiotics.

The guided tour, led by the laboratory's technical staff, gives access to the valuable collection of materials and instruments.

Over two floors, the historic building displays rooms and machinery from the early 20th century: equipment used to monitor hygiene and public healthcare, with particular attention to dietary irregularities and adulterations, water analyses and livestock controls, as well as the disinfection of objects, clothing, furniture and vehicles belonging to anyone who had contracted an infectious disease. The patio to the rear with its cast-iron gates was where cars and vans were treated; it now serves as storage space.

The laboratory (built in 1912) was designed by City Council architect Antonio Arévalo in an eclectic style between historicism and modernism.

Arévalo was also responsible for such diverse works as Bar España in Calle San Fernando, the El Progreso Industrial factory on Avenida Luis Montoto, and the network of neo-Mudéjar electricity substations (see p. 42) scattered across the centre and the Triana district.

Today the laboratory continues to be fully active in the field of public healthcare, undertaking clinical and epidemiological analyses and quality-control and public health checks.

The street adjacent to the centre, Calle Doctor Relimpio, owes its name to Federico Relimpio, its first director, a doctor and science professor, who died in 1919.

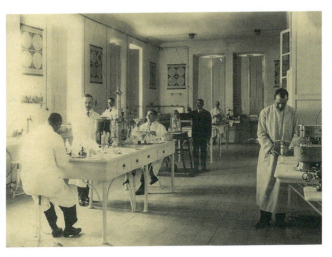

LILLIPUTIAN TRAIN

28

Railway from the 1929 Expo

Santa Justa train station: between tracks 8 and 9, level 0
asaf.es
Tuesday 7.30pm–9pm
Admission free

Hidden on level 0 of Santa Justa train station, between tracks 8 and 9 and behind the escalator, this Lilliputian locomotive was a key means of transport at the 1929 Ibero-American Exposition.

This fair, which took place in Seville between May 1929 and June 1930 with the participation of Spain, the US, Portugal and the Latin American countries, led to a huge level of urban development in the

southern part of the city, covering an area of 135 hectares. Having a miniature railway proved essential to getting around.

Built in 1928 by the Krauss company in Munich, Germany, it consisted of a locomotive weighing 10 tonnes and measuring 7.5 metres long by 1 metre wide, which could reach speeds of up to 30 km/h. Its water tank could hold 1,000 litres and it could carry up to 300 kg of coal, enough to drag the 10 carriages, each accommodating 16 people. Decorated in the colours of the Latin American republics, the carriages were divided into four compartments, each seating four passengers.

To start with, three locomotives and thirty carriages were purchased. The locomotives were christened with the names of Christopher Colombus' caravels: *La Pinta*, *La Niña* and *La Santa María*. Shortly afterwards, a fourth was bought, which was named *Sevilla*.

This attraction was a real tourist hit, making a one-way trip across its 5 km of train track through María Luisa park and past the pavilions. There were six stations, starting with the Bécquer roundabout and then stopping at Delicias, Galerías Comerciales, Barrio Moro, Parque de Atracciones and Plaza de América, going underneath Monte Gurugú via a purpose-built tunnel.

After the Expo closed, the trains were used intermittently until they fell into complete disrepair and were auctioned off in the 1930s. Of the four locomotives, one was scrapped while two others were rescued for use in theme parks in Ravenglass (UK) and Stuttgart (Germany). Fortune smiled on *La Niña*, which was renovated by the Asociación Sevillana de Amigos del Ferrocarril (Seville Association of Friends of the Railway) and may still be visited at Santa Justa station, surrounded by high-speed trains.

Monte Gurugú was built to commemorate the hill just outside the city of Melilla, the backdrop to terrible scenes of conflict in the early 20th century between Spanish troops and Abd el-Krim's Riffian rebels.

EQUESTRIAN STATUE:
THE EXPLORER

A Native American to commemorate the twinning of Seville and Kansas City

Corner of Avenida de Kansas City and Calle Samaniego

One of the city's most unusual urban features is found at the back of Santa Justa train station – the statue of a Native American on horseback, surveying the horizon and shielding his eyes from the Sun as

he looks towards the El Greco district. Although local wits have argued that he's looking towards the old Cruzcampo beer factory, you have to go back to 1922 to understand what a Native American is doing on an avenue in Seville.

That year, the Kansas City (Missouri) real-estate promoter J.C. Nichols visited Seville and, impressed by what he'd seen, went home with the idea of using Andalusian-style decorative and engineering features in the design of what was probably the world's first shopping centre, the Country Club Plaza, which opened its doors to the public in 1923.

Although Nichols originally intended to include such recognisable elements as the Giralda or the fountain in Plaza Virgen de los Reyes, this didn't happen until 1967, by which time he had died. Two years later Seville and Kansas City were twinned. This explains why the last stretch of what had previously been known as the San Pablo highway was renamed Avenida de Kansas City. Soon afterwards, a monolith with the Kansas City coat of arms was installed.

The current monument – the equestrian statue known as *The Explorer* – was erected on the remains of the old monolith.

Based on an original work by American sculptor Cyrus Edwin Dallin, it portrays a Native American explorer on horseback. The statue was exhibited at Seville's Expo '92 and was subsequently gifted to the city. It is a half-size replica of Dallin's 6-metre-high statue *The Scout*, erected in Kansas City as a permanent monument to the indigenous communities.

This sculpture (designed in 1910) was displayed at the 1915 Panama-Pacific International Exposition in San Francisco, where it won a gold medal.

Native Americans in Kansas

The US state of Kansas was home to many Native American peoples, and from 1829 it took in numerous communities that had been expelled from other states. Although they were assured that they would not be moved on again, that promise was broken after the Civil War. Currently there are four reservations for tribal nations in the state of Kansas: Iowa, Kickapoo, Potawatomi and Sac, and Fox.

Centro, Alfalfa and Museo

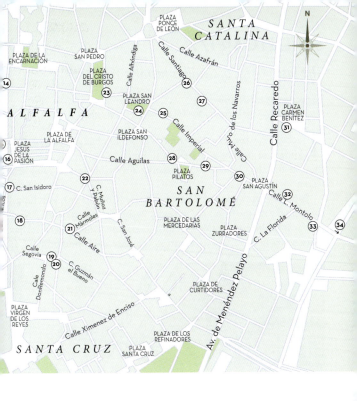

STREETCAR 177

The last vestige of Seville's historic trams

Bus station (Plaza de Armas)
Puente del Cristo de la Expiración (El Cachorro) (no number)

Tucked away between the platforms of Seville's bus station, and only known to passengers travelling to outlying towns, the last active tram in the city, *Tranvía 177*, is resting after a lifetime of toing and froing.

Popularly known as the *Tranvía de Coria* (Coria Tram), as it linked the capital with the towns of Coria and Puebla del Río, its route started not far from here, alongside Barranco market on Calle Arjona. Its first journey was in 1932, and its last on 18 February 1965, thus bringing an

end to the history of Seville's trams.

The first trams were run by the English Seville Tramways Company and started operations in 1887. They were known as *ferrocarriles de sangre* (blood railways) as they were pulled by mules. Their main stop was on Plaza de San Francisco, from where six lines radiated out, heading towards Macarena, Puerta Osario, Triana, Puerta Real, Calzada and Parque-Delicias.

Following the arrival of electricity, the first electric current traction lines were opened in 1899 – they stirred up controversy, and in some cases fierce opposition, from the outset. After a number of accidents, and with all the dangers involved in running through the narrow streets, the press started to refer to the tram system as the *peligro amarillo* (yellow peril).

In the early 20th century, a route opened up from Macarena to the cemetery: this black tram was No. 13.

Poor management and ongoing labour issues plunged the tram system into a crisis from which there was no coming back. The introduction of buses in the 1950s, considered a symbol of modernity,

was the trigger that led the City Council to decommission the urban tram network.

After years of neglect, trams did not return to Seville until 2007, when the Metrocentro was introduced between Plaza Nueva and the Prado de San Sebastián.

Not much remains of the tram system

Although most of the tram network has been removed, some vestiges remain: at the entrance to the San Fernando cemetery, on Calle Hernando Colón and in Plaza San Martín de Porres; and just the one stop, on the Heliópolis roundabout, currently used by the bus. The sign for an old tram stop has also survived on Calle Betis (see p. 215).

There's another tram carriage, from route 314, in the Triana district on Plaza de San Martín de Porres – it was renovated in 2005.

ATLAS FIGURES ON THE DOME OF THE CHURCH OF LA MAGDALENA

The secret of the indigenous warriors

Church of La Magdalena, Corner of Calle Bailén and Calle Murillo

If you look up at the rooftop of the church of La Magdalena from the corner of Calle Murillo and Calle Bailén, you'll see some surprising Atlas figures: eight powerful Amerindian warriors holding up the cupola of the dome, each with a blue Sun at his feet. At the corners of the roof of the tower, you'll also spot indigenous masks in glazed polychrome tilework casting a mocking look over the Seville roof terraces.

These figures are reminiscent of the famous colossal Toltec Atlantean figures from Tula, which keep guard over the temples, alluding to the civilisation's fallen warriors, and whose mission was to accompany the Sun on its heavenly course.

In its financial and social heyday, Seville alternated constantly between two continents as it was the headquarters of Casa de la Contratación de las Indias (House of Trade of the Indies), which was in charge of overseas commerce between 1503 and 1717.

The church of La Magdalena was built over the ruins of the Gothic-Mudéjar church of the monastery of San Pablo – the biggest Dominican monastery in Andalusia – which housed many monks before they set sail to evangelise the Americas and the Philippines. The first Dominican mission arrived at La Española (Santo Domingo) in September 1510. They reached Mexico in 1526, in the midst of Hernán Cortés' war with the Mexican empire. Some of these missions to the Indies were organised by the Dominican Bartolomé de las Casas, known as the 'defender of the Indians of the New World'. He was named bishop at this monastery and ordained bishop of Chiapas (Mexico) in 1543.

Leonardo de Figueroa

The commission to build the Baroque church of La Magdalena went to Seville's most prominent architect of the day, Leonardo de Figueroa (Utiel, Valencia, c. 1654 – Seville, 1730). He completed it in 1709. Figueroa was the architect behind such major works in the city as the church of San Luis, the palace of San Telmo, the church of El Salvador and the Hospital de La Caridad.

ORDEALS OF DIEGO DURO

A reminder of the Spanish Inquisition

Calle Bailén, 5
Church of La Magdalena
Nave of the Epistle side
Monday & Friday 7.45am–11am, 6.30pm–9pm; Tuesday, Wednesday,
Thursday & Saturday 7.45am–1.30pm, 6.30pm–9pm; Sunday & bank holidays
8.45am–2pm, 6.30pm–9pm

A shocking scene is depicted in the large-scale mural painting to the right of the transept in the church of La Magdalena. A man condemned to death by the Inquisition is riding a little grey donkey and wearing the full Sanbenito attire of the penitent: a yellowish sackcloth with the cross of St Andrew and a tall paper cap with drawings of the flames that await him at his death. The procession is moving slowly, surrounded by a jeering mob, accompanied by Dominican monks and soldiers, and followed by a figure dressed in ermine cloak and crown and carrying fuel for the fire. This is King Ferdinand III of Castile, the conqueror of Seville.

The date was 28 October 1703 and the *auto-da-fé* had just condemned Diego Duro, a tradesman from Osuna, to the severest punishment for practising Judaism: to be burned at the stake on the Holy Inquisition's pyre on the Prado de San Sebastián.

Seville painter Lucas Valdés executed this fresco just two years later, while architect Leonardo de Figueroa was completing work on the Baroque church being built on the ruins of the Gothic-Mudéjar church belonging to the monastery of San Pablo el Real. The monastery stood on land donated by King Ferdinand III to the Dominicans (who gave support to his army in the conquest of the city) and is where the present-day church and the neighbouring Hotel Colón now stand.

The mural was destroyed in 1813, while there were still monks living in the monastery, and was only restored in 1982.

The Holy Office started working in Seville in 1481, hunting down Judaising practices by converted Jews and heretics. As the Dominican Order was in charge of this task, the monastery of San Pablo became the Inquisition's first headquarters in Spain and housed its first prison cells. In February that year, the Quemadero de Tablada was inaugurated with the execution of six people. Three years later, Seville was where the sinister Torquemada's first rules of the Inquisition were approved. Although lack of space meant that within a few years the Inquisition's headquarters moved to the castle of San Jorge in Triana (see p. 206), many of the most solemn *autos-da-fé* continued to be carried out at the monastery.

In the niche over the outside door, St Dominic can be seen guarded by dogs with torches in their jaws, lighting up the globe of the world. These are the *domini canis*, the dogs of the Lord.

ROYAL TIMBER WAREHOUSE

*From the forests of Segura and down the
Guadalquivir river*

Corner of Calle Arjona and Calle Segura

Before crossing Triana bridge, opposite Barranco market, stands a curious white building in Baroque style – the ground floor now houses a car dealership. Few of the many passers-by know that this building was a major 18th-century Seville institution: the Real Negociado de Maderas de Sevilla (Seville's Royal Timber Department).

Built in 1735, the original building that stored the king's wood corresponds to the ground floor of the current edifice. Its great brick walls and characteristic watchtowers at the four corners give it a military and colonial air. In 1958 two upper floors were added to provide housing, and during the 1960s a bus station was installed inside, mainly with routes to Huelva.

The Real Negociado was set up to manage the large quantities of wood required to build the Real Fábrica de Tabacos (Royal Tobacco Factory), today's Seville University (see p. 238). It was decided to source this timber from the Sierra de Segura in Jaén, thereby avoiding the long journey from Flanders. Ferdinand VI subsequently created the maritime province of Segura, decreeing that the resources of large forested areas – mainly in the mountainous Sierra regions of Jaén and Albacete – should be used to construct ships for the royal navy, including vessels for the Indies fleets.

In 1734 the first shipment of timber arrived, consisting of over 8,000 pieces of top-quality black pine. From then on, once a year during the winter months when the water levels were high, logs were transported down the Guadalimar and Guadalquivir rivers to Seville and, subsequently, to La Carraca arsenal in San Fernando (Cádiz).

The highly challenging job of steering the timber was carried out by a group of up to 300 river pilots called *gancheros*, with those from Priego de Córdoba being the most highly prized. The logs could be up to 30 metres long and it took between seven and ten months to travel the 400 km to their destination in Seville.

Faded plaque from 1812
On one side of the building is an old stone plaque whose text has largely worn away. However, it's possible to make out the following words: '*On the twenty-eighth of August eighteen hundred and twelve was held in this ...*', referring to the events held to celebrate the end of French rule after the Peninsular War.

CHAPEL OF SAN ONOFRE

The hermit's hidden oratory

Plaza Nueva, 3
Open 24 hours a day, 365 days a year

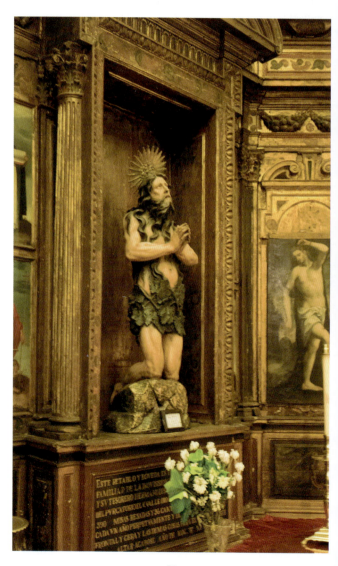

Co\
oncealed behind the façade of a building in the Regionalist style, the chapel of San Onofre doesn't attract a second glance, despite being the last remains of the great convent of San Francisco, dating back to the 13th century. After falling into complete disrepair, it was demolished in 1840, making way for today's Plaza Nueva.

The chapel was founded in 1520 by the Hermandad de las Ánimas (Brotherhood of Souls) for the purpose of praying for the souls of those in purgatory. It is dedicated to the eccentric 4th-century hermit Onuphrius, seen praying to the heavens under his great mane of hair from the altarpiece created by sculptor Martínez Montañés.

The hermit lived in the Egyptian desert, where he survived on dates (as well as the bread and wine provided by an angel, according to legend), clothed in nothing but palm leaves and his own flowing mane of hair.

NEARBY
Seven-headed cross
Arquillo *(little archway), Seville Town Hall*
Plaza de San Francisco

Imitating the town hall's Renaissance decoration, next to the *arquillo* and alongside the lower chapterhouse, the seven-headed cross refers to its seven angels. Executed in 1903, the cross replaces a simpler one erected 200 years earlier to mark the last *auto-da-fé* held by the Inquisition in Plaza de San Francisco. The Franciscan symbol of the five wounds may be seen above the Renaissance arch that served as an entrance to the convent's front patio.

End of the Inquisition

Spain's last sentence to death by burning was carried out in Seville in 1781. The hapless victim was an elderly blind woman called María Dolores López, popularly known as 'Beata Dolores' (Holy Dolores), who was accused of heresy and condemned to burn on the Prado de San Sebastián pyre – exactly three centuries after the first immolations in 1481.

The end of the Inquisition arrived thanks to Napoleon in 1808 and the Courts of Cádiz in 1813. And, though Ferdinand VII reinstated the Holy Office, it was abolished for good in 1834.

PLUS ULTRA RELIEF

The motto of a boundless empire

Seville Town Hall
Plaza de San Francisco, next to the arquillo *arch*

Next to the town hall *arquillo*, and on the door to the lower chapter house, is one of the oldest known representations of the motto *Plus Ultra* ('Further Beyond' in a literal translation of the Latin).

The relief on the Renaissance-style stone façade shows two pillars topped by crowns and entwined in a banner on which the motto is engraved, all on a base of ocean waves. The same symbol may also be found engraved towards the top of the extremely fine wooden door to the lower chapter house. In this case, each pillar is being pushed towards the centre by a straining Hercules figure.

In 1532 work began on the reliefs on the façade of the town hall,

a building project promoted by Charles V following marriage to his cousin, Isabella of Portugal. The nuptials took place in Seville in 1526 and the king was shocked that the most prominent civic building in what was then considered the capital city of the known world was such an inferior and undistinguished edifice. Only 10 years earlier, the emperor had included the *Plus Ultra* motto on the imperial coat of arms as a representation of his power and the wide reach of his empire.

The emblem refers to Hercules, considered one of the founders of the city of Seville. In one of his labours, he is said to have separated two enormous pillars, identified as two opposing rocky mountains, Gibraltar in the south of Spain and possibly Jebel Musa in northern Morocco. As such, the Strait of Gibraltar marked the end of the known world, with the legend *Non Terrae Plus Ultra* (No Lands Further Beyond) warning sailors that if they passed that point, they would be met with a host of marine monsters and enormous abysses and waterfalls.

But when Columbus discovered the Americas – and, years later, Juan Sebastián Elcano became the first to circumnavigate the globe, completing the expedition started by Magellan (see p. 216) – this put an end to the mythological hero's warning message. Only the *Plus Ultra* motto remained, as a sign to the world that you could indeed venture beyond that point.

Esoteric meaning?

As Plato noted, for a boat coming from the Mediterranean to go beyond the pillars of Hercules – symbolically positioned in the Strait of Gibraltar – it had to be heading for the mythical land of Atlantis: for some people, the location of secret knowledge. As such, the symbol of the twin pillars has long guarded access to the unknown. Going beyond them means leaving the material realm behind and entering the sphere of enlightenment.

Thus the entrance to the temple of Jerusalem also featured two bronze pillars, known as Jachin and Boaz, which were the inspiration for the two pillars at the entrance to Masonic Temples.

Origin of the dollar sign

One of the most widespread theories about the origin of the $ sign holds that this was a stylisation of the pillars of Hercules that appeared on gold bars and coins produced at the Mexican *Ceca* (Mint). So the banner with the motto *Plus Ultra* is the S, while the pillars are the two vertical bars.

'NO8DO' SYMBOL
AT THE TOWN HALL

*'It hasn't abandoned me', or the knot of the union of
the empire*

Seville Town Hall
Plaza Nueva, 1
sevilla.org/actualidad/visitas-casa-consistorial
Monday–Thursday: free admission for those born or living in Seville
Saturday: free admission for the general public

On the frieze at the southern end of the lower chapter house of Seville Town Hall – in two cartouches flanked by sculptural groups depicting Calvary and the sacrifice of Isaac, and alongside the spectacular dome decorated with reliefs of Castilian and Leonese monarchs – is the oldest surviving version of the city's symbol par excellence, dating to approximately 1533. This symbol is made up of two syllables in capital letters, NO and DO, joined by an 8 in the form of a knotted skein of yarn. Few cities can boast a logo that has officially identified them for at least five centuries and possibly quite a bit longer.

With very little historical basis, Seville locals have been handing down a mythical explanation to the riddle behind this logo from generation to generation. According to their version, the puzzle may be solved with a literal translation both memorable and easy to understand. As the story goes, Seville was one of the few cities that remained loyal to Alfonso X in the 1283 war of succession that pitted him against his son Sancho, who enjoyed the support of many of the nobles and the king's wife herself, Doña Violante. So the king is supposed to have referred to the city with the words '*No me ha dejado*' (It hasn't abandoned me), which was then transformed into *no-madeja-do*, with (*madeja* meaning 'skein'). This explains the symbolic use of the figure 8 to represent the knotted yarn. Alfonso died a few months later and was succeeded by his son despite having disinherited him.

But the most surprising thing is that this bizarre explanation did not turn up until the 17th century, though there are records of the symbol going back at least two centuries earlier.

The alternative (and more realistic) explanation is linked to Alfonso X's legitimate claim to the throne of the Holy Roman Empire after the death of his grandfather, Frederick II. A claim he would continue to press for more than half his reign without the slightest success. In this case, the origin of the *Nodo* motto is directly related to the etymological Latin root *nodus* (knot), reinforced by the 8 that is directly reminiscent of the mythical value of the Herculean knot ... the knot with which the wise king was setting out to unite the empire.

GRACE KELLY MEDALLION

Stories from the façade of the town hall

Seville Town Hall
Plaza de San Francisco

On the façade of Seville Town Hall, jostling with imperial coats of arms, statues of Hercules and Julius Caesar, and stone reliefs of mythological animals, there is a surprising relief of Grace Kelly sculpted inside the medallion under the penultimate central window. But how did an image of the Hitchcock muse end up here?

Work on the Renaissance town hall got under way in 1526, to a design by architect Diego de Riaño. That year, Seville was chosen as the venue for the marriage of Charles V to Isabella of Portugal, taking on the prominent mantle of imperial capital. The magnificent stone building, two storeys high, took almost half a century to complete. The Renaissance building occupies one third of the left-hand side of the current edifice, including the *arquillo* (little arch), that led to what was once the convent of San Francisco. Centuries passed before extension works were undertaken on a building that was clearly no longer large enough to meet the city's needs. In 1868 Demetrio de los Ríos was commissioned to build the new façade, which was supposed to follow the plateresque style of the old town hall. Although sculptor Pedro Domínguez started the carvings on the façade in 1890, the work dragged on for almost a century, passing from one sculptor to the next until it was abandoned in the 1970s, with the relief stone carving left as seen today. The last in this long line of stone carvers was Manuel Echegoyán. Born in Espartinas (Seville) in 1905, from an early age he excelled as a master sculptor, creating the monument to Emilio Castelar (president of the First Spanish Republic) in the Cristina gardens when just 25. He became Professor of Drawing at the San Fernando Academy in Madrid, which was where he was when the uprising against the Republic broke out. During the Civil War he worked as a topographer for the army and was imprisoned in Madrid until, in 1940, he returned to Seville, where he was barred from practising his profession. Over the years, Echegoyán regained his prestige and was commissioned to complete this neo-plateresque façade. It so happened that in 1966 the actress Grace Kelly visited the city's Feria de Abril (Seville Fair) with her husband, Prince Rainier of Monaco. It was thus that Echegoyán decided to use her as a model for one of the medallions.

Self-portrait of the sculptor and his wife

The relief of Grace Kelly was Echegoyán's penultimate female figure; the last was the effigy of his wife, opposite a profile of the sculptor, who carved his self-portrait for posterity ... an exercise in poetic justice.

A trip back in time

Calle Sierpes, 40
954 56 47 71
maquedano.com
Monday–Friday 10am–2pm & 6pm–9pm, Saturday 10am–2pm

The tiny modernist premises spread over three floors at No. 40 Calle Sierpes have housed one of the city's oldest and most charming shops since the beginning of the 20th century.

With its hundreds of elegant round hat boxes stacked up precariously and even going up the spiral staircase, the Maquedano hat shop invites you to travel back in time. Look out for its great mirror, high moulded ceilings, display window with the founder's initials engraved on the glass, exquisite tiled borders and wood and brass shop sign. One of the oldest millineries in Spain, it was founded in 1896 and has continued operating without a break since 1908 on these very premises, the work of architect José Gómez Millán.

The first floor, now used as storage, housed the workshop where the hatters and lining experts plied their trade.

Even today you can still find Andalusian hats alongside classic models: Panama hats, straw hats, fedoras, trilbies, flat caps and sun hats ...

NEARBY

Salón Llorens

Calle Sierpes, 26

Inside the Salón Llorens video games arcade, much of the neo-Mudéjar architecture of the old Llorens Cinema still survives, designed in 1913 by Regionalist architect José Espiau.

This venue became a fashionable spot for high-class Seville society, acting as theatre, cinema and concert hall. The great pianist Arthur Rubinstein and the classical guitar player Andrés Segovia both performed here.

LIBRERIÁ VERBO

The only European bookstore located in a theatre

Calle Sierpes, 25
Monday–Saturday 10am–8pm

Strange how few Seville locals know Verbo Bookstore on Calle Sierpes in spite of its vast area (covering 1,400 square metres). It also has the unusual feature of being housed inside the old Imperial Theatre, which first opened its doors in 1906, seating almost a thousand, and closed in 1999. After remaining vacant for several years, it was converted into a bookstore between 2004 and 2014, finally opening its doors in 2017.

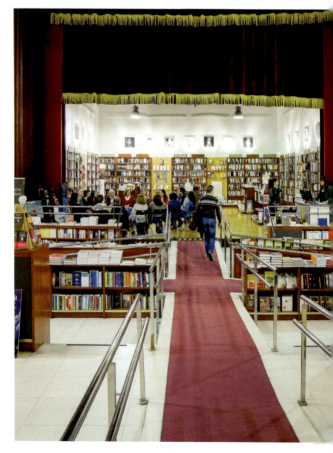

The bookstore occupies the entire space of the theatre, from foyer to stalls, amphitheatre to stage. Following its renovation the old stage machinery was recovered, along with the mouldings and iron fixings that secured the footlights to the stage. High up, in what used to be the gods, there's still a booth with two old cinema projectors.

The theatre was built on the site of an old convent that was disentailed in the 19th century. It started out as a café with live entertainment, featuring vedettes, dancers, flamenco singers and so on, all performing late into the night.

For many years it was an iconic spot on Seville's cultural scene, with a film programme ranging from early silent movies to the golden age of American cinema, as well as plays by authors as diverse as Shakespeare and the Álvarez Quintero brothers.

The most beautiful bookstore in the world

Ateneo Grand Splendid in Buenos Aires (Argentina), considered the most beautiful bookstore in the world, stands on the site of another old theatre (see *Secret Buenos Aires*, by the same publisher).

NEARBY

Papelería Ferrer: the oldest stationers in Spain and the third oldest in Europe   ⑫

Calle Sierpes, 5
954 22 64 14 – papeleriaferrer.es
Monday–Friday 10am–2pm & 5pm–8.30pm, Saturday 10am–2pm

Almost at the beginning of Calle Sierpes, Papelería Ferrer is the oldest stationers in Spain and the third oldest in Europe. Walking inside is like entering a living museum of writing and classical stationery – giving a foretaste in the overflowing shop windows and the sign written in old-fashioned calligraphy, revealing that the business was established in 1856. Inside, the period counters and shelves have countless articles on display: writing implements, fountain pens and inks, the most beautiful Hungarian writing paper, handmade French bindings, leather and bronze-covered diaries, goose quills ... all under the watchful eyes of the fifth generation of the Ferrer family. Their forebears opened this business in Seville in the mid-19th century when they missed the ship to Venezuela, where they were intending to embark on a new life.

PLAQUE ON LUIS CERNUDA'S HOUSE

The poet who never returned from exile

Calle Acetres, 6

"RECUERDO AQUEL RINCÓN DEL PATIO EN LA CASA NATAL. YO A SOLAS Y SENTADO EN EL PRIMER PELDAÑO DE LA ESCALERA DE MÁRMOL. LA VELA ESTABA ECHADA. SUMIENDO EL AMBIENTE EN UNA FRESCA PENUMBRA. Y SOBRE LA LONA. POR DONDE SE FILTRABA TAMIZADA LA LUZ DEL MEDIODÍA. UNA ESTRELLA DESTACABA SUS SEIS PUNTAS DE PAÑO ROJO"

OCNOS "EL TIEMPO"

A LUIS CERNUDA. EN EL CENTENARIO DE SU NACIMIENTO. SEVILLA. 2002

Akey figure from the so-called Generation of '27, Luis Cernuda – one of Seville's major poets – was born in a house in the maze that is the historic centre, very close to Calle Cuna. To mark this, a plaque on the wall gives his date of birth, 21 September 1902, and a fragment from his prose poem *El Tiempo* (Time): 'I remember that corner of the patio in the house where I was born, all by myself and sitting on the bottom step of the marble staircase ...' Thanks to a public campaign, the building was granted protected heritage status, saving it from oblivion and ruin.

This was a typical middle-class, one-family Seville home from the period, with three floors arranged around a patio. It goes down in history not only as the house where the poet was born but also for having inspired *Ocnos*, one of his seminal works.

Cernuda's years in this house left a profound mark on him. Nostalgia for the places of his childhood is reflected in the different parts of the building, on both a physical and spiritual level – the patio as the ecosystem of his memories, the roof terrace where the summer evenings unfold, the balconies from where the life outside could be glimpsed, the fountain, the bedrooms, the hallway ... All these images pour melancholically into *Ocnos*, his mature collection issued by The Dolphin publishers in London in 1942 and including 31 poems written over the two previous years.

Cernuda spent his childhood here until 1914, when his strict military father was posted to the Zapadores barracks in the Porvenir district. On his death in 1920, the family returned to the city centre, to a little house on Calle del Aire, very close to the Roman columns of Calle Mármoles (see p. 102). In 1938 Cernuda was forced into exile from a country ravaged by the Civil War. He had been actively involved in defending the Republican government, even fighting in the Alpine battalion in the Sierra de Guadarrama (Madrid). Nostalgia for his homeland and a sense of rejection because of his homosexuality would plague him throughout an exile from which he never returned: after some years in England, he moved to the US and finally Mexico, where he died in 1963. His remains are buried there in the cemetery of the Panteón Jardín (Pantheon Garden).

'There are human destinies linked to a place or a landscape': so wrote the poet who never returned to Seville ... and who would never forget the city.

Advertising by the man who introduced Colombian coffee to Spain

Calle Goyeneta, 9

One of the best examples of commercial advertising from the first half of the 20th century lies hidden in the maze of streets in the city centre. No. 9, Calle Goyeneta, built in a neo-Baroque style in 1925, was home to the offices and coffee roasters of Café Saimaza, one of Seville's most iconic brands.

The façades have two identical pairs of blue-and-white ceramic panels, the work of the famous Triana ceramics factory, Mensaque – they show scenes of a colonial nature where coffee is being planted, harvested and served, under a banner with the owner's name. We also find the motto *aroma concentrado* (concentrated aroma), a slogan that was replaced in later years by *el café de los cafeteros* (the coffee of coffee-lovers).

The Saimaza brand name was taken from the surname of Joaquín Sainz de la Maza, a Cantabrian-born entrepreneur who started a coffee business in the Andalusian capital in 1908. Just 25 years later, he would figure as the country's third-largest importer of coffee beans and the man who introduced Colombian coffee to Spain.

The brand stopped production in Seville in 2013.

Seville's ceramic advertising heritage

Seville was a historical benchmark in the manufacture of ceramics, a large part of which was destined for trade and advertising. The thirty or so painted tile advertisements that still survive today are an anthropological snapshot of the customs and habits of days past, as well as having great artistic value. The city's ceramic advert par excellence is the *Studebaker* sign (Calle Tetuán, 9), painted by Enrique Orce Mármol in 1924 for the factory belonging to the widow and children of Ramos Rejano. In addition to the signs on Calle Alfarería in Triana, where the Centro de la Cerámica (Ceramics Centre, see p. 100) is located, another piece worth mentioning is by Mensaque for *Seguros Velázquez*, and one for *Armería Z* by José Ruesga in 1945, both on Calle Sierpes; the advertisements on the façade of Los Claveles bar (Plaza de los Terceros); and perhaps one of the oldest and most iconic works, the *Alegoría del comercio*, painted by José Recio in around 1915 (Calle Rioja, 1).

COLUMNS IN THE PATIO OF THE OLD MOSQUE OF IBN ADABBÁS

A sacred memory

Calle Córdoba, 3
iglesiasalvador.es
Guided tour of the crypt and roofs: engranajesculturales.com

On the right of the bell tower of the church of El Salvador, a little passageway leads to a secluded patio surrounded by arches supported by 10 columns with Roman and Visigothic capitals. The columns are buried up to the middle, bearing witness to the original level of the patio, some 3 metres lower than today. This would have been the old ritual ablutions patio (*sahn*) of the mosque of Ibn Adabbás.

Built by the Islamic *qadi* (judge) Ibn Adabbás in 829, it was Seville's most important mosque until the Great Mosque was inaugurated in 1182 on the site where the cathedral now stands. Just 14 years after it was founded, in the mid-9th century, the mosque of Ibn Adabbás

was set fire to by Vikings who sailed up the Guadalquivir and attacked Seville.

After the Christian conquest of the 13th century, the best-preserved mosques were handed over to the Church.

The mosque underwent certain minor decorative modifications, and for four centuries was used as the church of the Divino Salvador, until it was demolished in 1671 after falling into disrepair.

The building of the current Baroque church was completed in 1712 under the supervision of architect Leonardo de Figueroa.

Other vestiges of the mosque

In the patio, the lower part of the bell tower of the church of El Salvador corresponds to the minaret of the mosque, which lost its upper part in the earthquake of 1356.

The two outstanding bronze knockers from the mosque's main door are now on the door of the exhibition room of the Hermandad Sacramental del Salvador, located in the same patio. Each hexagonal knocker is held in the jaws of a feline whose head rests on an octagonal pyramid-shaped moulding, attached to the door by a starred polygon.

We can be certain about the year the mosque was built due to the oldest known Arabic inscription from Al Andalus, which can still be seen on the mosque's foundation column. This greenish-grey marble shaft originated from some Roman building. After the Castilian conquest, it was Christianised by the engraving of an anagram featuring a cross over a globe of the world, and remained in the prayer room until the building was demolished. The column is now on display in the Museo Arqueológico (Museum of Archaeology), finally at rest after so many vicissitudes.

The interesting tour of the crypt of the church of El Salvador includes the ashlars of the columns of the mosque. The most important piece in this room is a plaque that was originally set into the tower,

with an inscription that mentions the renovation works undertaken by the poet king al-Mu'tamid following the 1079 earthquake. In the nearby Plaza del Pan (see p. 92), market stalls were attached to the walls of the mosque – over the years, they have become the little shops of today, some of which still have columns of Roman origin from the Islamic building.

COLUMNS IN PLAZA DEL PAN

Echoes of the old Islamic souk

Plaza de Jesús de la Pasión

Adjoining the back wall of the church of El Salvador is a series of tiny shops under a vaulted arcade supported by 22 marble columns of Roman and Visigothic origin. They come from the old mosque of Ibn Adabbás (see p. 90), which reused these elements when it was built in the 9th century.

In fact, this whole area was part of the old Roman forum, centred around the nearby Plaza de la Alfalfa, which was the scene of great commercial activity – this intensified in the Islamic period, when the souk was annexed to the mosque that gave rise to this square.

Following the Christian conquest in the 13th century, the square took the name of Plaza de los Poyos de las Hogazas and Plaza de las Tahonas, in clear allusion to the manufacture of bread (*hogazas* = loaves and *tahonas* = bakeries), but it wasn't until the 17th century that it adopted the name by which it is popularly known: Plaza del Pan (Bread Square).

It was home to the bakers of Alcalá de Guaraíra and Los Alcores. In his *Letters from Spain*, writer Blanco White describes the bustle of activity witnessed in the late 18th century: 'Some 60 men and double that number of mules leave Alcalá every day heading for Seville, where they remain until late in Plaza del Pan ...'

The mosque wall

Inside the shop at No. 11 in the square, you can still see the original wall of Ibn Adabbás' mosque: at floor level is a small elongated window protruding from the rest of the building, buried some 3 metres down. The square's original Renaissance floor can be seen through the glass floor of the shop at No. 13.

Medieval guilds in Seville street names

The souk spread out over the current Plaza del Pan, Plaza del Salvador and Plaza de la Alfalfa. Nearby Calle Alcaicería is derived from an old Arab *alcaicería*, or market selling consumer goods, along with health and hygiene products. Today's street names, including Lineros, Boteros, Herbolario and Cedaceros, bear witness to the importance of trades and guilds (in this case, makers or sellers of linen, boots, herbs, wineskins and fishing nets). Shoemakers (*zapateros*), in particular, have survived to the present day. In fact, in the 16th century Calle Córdoba was known as Zapateros de lo Viejo.

CURRO'S ROCKING MACHINE

*The last mascot still on show from the 1992
Universal Exposition*

*Jardilín
Calle Francos, 15
Monday–Saturday 10am–9pm*

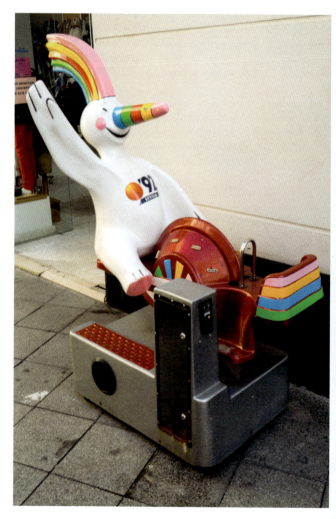

Every day except Sunday, at 10am, the owners of Jardilín – a shop selling babies' and children's clothes since 1968 – take out the rocking machine ridden by Curro, the last mascot still on show from Seville's 1992 Universal Exposition. Living on in the memories of all Seville locals of a certain age, the icon created by Czech designer Heinz Edelmann (1934–2009) as the symbol of Expo '92 takes pride of place. Edelmann was known the world over for his art direction and character designs for the film *Yellow Submarine* (1966), where this magician of psychedelic pop drew the most famous caricatures of the Beatles.

Curro was a white dinosaurian with elephant feet, a big crest and an enormous conical nose, both rainbow-coloured in reference to the five continents. The mascot had a huge impact, becoming an extremely popular icon used in all sorts of marketing products, such as this rocking toy, so it's not unusual to see passers-by taking photos of it for old times' sake.

Retirement of the mascot

Retired from the game and put out to pasture like stars of the stage after their hectic lives, over a hundred Curros lie dormant in an antiques warehouse in Alcalá de Guadaíra (Seville). These rocking machines, which still work, can be bought from the Romano Antigüedades company, along with numerous decorative items from Expo '92, which were purchased in the great auction that took place once the Exposition had ended.

CROMBERGER'S STONE PLAQUE

The place where the first printing press set sail for the Americas

Calle Pajaritos, 7

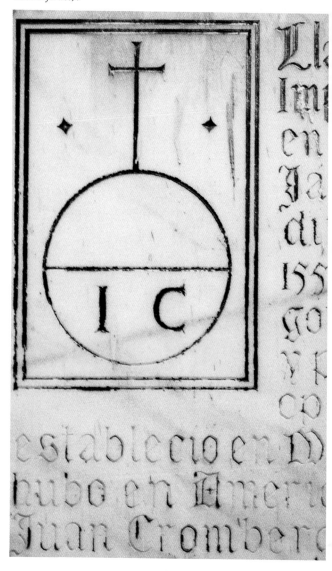

On an old stone plaque at No. 7 Calle Pajaritos, you'll see some text with a globe (symbolising the world), crowned by a cross with the initials IC. It commemorates the fact that in the 16th century one of the most important printing presses in the whole of Spain departed from here, headed for the New World. IC (standing for Imprenta Cromberger) is a reference to the German Jacob Cromberger, who set up his print workshop here in 1511. Known from then on as Calle de la Imprenta (Printing Press Street), in the 17th century it changed its name to Calle Pajaritos in reference to a well-known tavern mentioned by Tirso de Molina in his famous play, *El Burlador de Sevilla* (The Trickster of Seville).

With the founding of Seville's Casa de Contratación (House of Trade) in 1503, which regulated all commerce and navigation with Spain's overseas territories, the city became a major communications hub.

One year earlier Jacob Cromberger, a native of Nuremberg, had set himself up in the city as a printer, publisher and bookseller: in 1502 he printed *The Tragicomedy of Calisto and Melibea*, an incredibly popular work by Fernando de Rojas. This heralded the start of a long line of great Seville printers of Germanic origin.

With his son, Juan, Cromberger senior specialised in all sorts of publications: small commissions, including loose pages, certificates, indulgences and unbound pamphlets such as those sold by the blind while they recited news and poems. But they also printed important volumes on religion, philosophy (including various works by the reformer Erasmus), poetry, history, medicine, navigation (such as the famous *Treatise on the Sphere and the Art of Sailing*) and chivalric romances (including *Amadís de Gaula*).

In 1525 father and son were granted a licence to export books to the New World, but it wasn't until June 1539 that they established their printing press in Mexico City, thanks to one of their machinists of Italian origin called Juan Pablos.

ORIENTAL ART COLLECTION IN CASA DE LOS PINELO

Japan and China in Seville

Real Academia de Bellas Artes de Santa Isabel de Hungría
Calle Abades, 14
954 21 22 98
rabasih@insacan.org
Monday–Friday 10.30am–2.30pm
Regular night tours

The extraordinary Renaissance townhouse known as the Casa de los Pinelo has one of the finest – and curiously little-known – collections of Japanese and Chinese art in Spain: more than 200 items, including paintings, sculptures, ceramics and silverware, mostly from the 18th and 19th centuries.

Prominent pieces include a bronze image of Kannon Bosatsu, with eight pairs of arms, which in Buddhism represents the search for supreme enlightenment, as well as a pair of bronze dragons (Ryu). It is also worth highlighting a number of Chinese paintings of great Taoist symbolism and influence, such as the 16th-century work by Chou Chimian entitled *Birds of Paradise and Flowers*. Japanese works include a page from the sketch album of Hokusai (1769–1849), internationally known for his *Great Wave*, a colourful Kabuki theatre scene from 1874 by Toyohara Kunichika (1835–1900), and a Shunrai painting of the Buddhist monk Daruma.

All these pieces were donated to Seville's Real Academia de Bellas Artes (Royal Academy of Fine Arts) by the Jesuit Fernando García Gutiérrez in 2002.

The Jesuits' link to Japan goes back several centuries, when their founder sailed to Japanese lands on an evangelical mission in 1549.

The samurai who came to stay for good

In December 1614, having made stops in Veracruz (Mexico) and Havana (Cuba), a galleon arrived in Seville carrying a diplomatic party from faraway Japan, led by the samurai Hasekura Tsunenaga, who was subsequently christened Felipe Francisco Faxecura. He brought a message of friendship addressed to Philip III on a roll of illustrated rice paper that is preserved in Seville's Archivo de Indias (Archive of the Indies). According to contemporary accounts, the expedition numbered: '30 men with blades, their captain of the guard, and 12 bowmen and halberdiers with painted spears'. The ship docked at Coria del Río, where they were met by representatives from the town council who accompanied them to Seville by land. The distinguished visitors 'never touched their food with their hands but used two little sticks which they held between three fingers', the records tell us. Some of the members of that expedition decided to stay in Coria, where their descendants (estimated to number some 700) have kept their Japanese surnames to this day, and there is a statue of a samurai gazing out over the river Guadalquivir.

OLAVIDE'S TILES

The enlightened dream of a great mayor of Seville

Corner of Calle Abades and Calle Segovia

The intersection where the Renaissance townhouse Casa de los Pinelo stands is a good place to admire a selection of the curious ceramic tiles (*azulejos*) that Pablo de Olavide, *asistente* (governor) of Seville, had installed in the late 18th century in an attempt to differentiate the various parts of the city.

Here the three types of Baroque street-markings can be seen: those that indicate the district, neighbourhood and block; those that refer to the name of the street or square (in this case, Calle Abades Alta); and, finally, those giving the house number.

All these ceramic tiles were individually made by craftsmen and had a white background with a cobalt blue frame; they featured a

Cross of Malta at the top and all used the same typography, executed in black, using manganese. Their clean, uniform design gives them a clearly modern feel. Sadly, of the thousands erected at the time, barely a hundred survive today.

The tiles reflect the modern, rational and enlightened town-planning that Olavide tried to introduce with the issue of a Royal Decree in 1769. They are directly linked to the first complete street map of the city of Seville, which he commissioned from the engineer Francisco Manuel Coelho in 1768 and was published in 1771.

Until then, the city had been organised in a fairly anarchic manner into so-called '*collaciones*', each one around its corresponding parish church, much as in medieval times. Olavide's innovative project, following Madrid's example, divided the city into five districts – A, B, C, D and Triana – each under the supervision of an *alcalde* (mayor). Each district was split up into eight neighbourhoods and these were then divided into blocks.

Pablo de Olavide

Pablo de Olavide y Jáuregui (1725–1803) was born in Lima (Peru), where as a young man he excelled in law and politics. In Paris, where he spent many years, he became acquainted with Voltaire and Diderot and soaked up all the new Enlightenment thought. In 1767 Charles III appointed him *asistente* (governor) of Seville, where he clashed with the city's more traditional elements. In 1778 he was condemned by the Inquisition and attempts were made to erase all his work from the city's memory: all the copies that could be found of his map of Seville were destroyed. Thankfully, in the early 20th century four copper plates of the map were discovered in a second-hand goods shop, being sold as scrap metal.

D. PABLO OLAVIDE.

ROMAN COLUMNS
ON CALLE MÁRMOLES

Where the Alameda de Hércules columns came from

Calle Mármoles, 1

At the intersection between Calle Mármoles and Calle Aire there are three 9-metre columns unexpectedly tucked away on a little plot of land surrounded by buildings. In the 16th century the remains of a Roman building were found here, including six granite columns on white marble bases.

Although the columns have traditionally been considered part of a temple or the entrance to a square, the function of the original building is still a mystery.

In 1574 two of the original six columns were removed and relocated to serve as an entrance to what were the first European public gardens: the Alameda de Hércules (see below). Removing and transporting the columns was a huge engineering challenge at the time ... 12 years before the Egyptian obelisk was erected in St Peter's Square in Rome. A third column broke while being moved to the Alcázar and is thought to be buried somewhere near the Giralda.

The three remaining columns were crammed into the patio of a private house until it was demolished by the Seville City Council at the end of the 19th century.

Roman columns originating from Turkey

The most surprising thing is the columns' place of origin: recent studies claim they came from the region of Troy, in modern-day Turkey, which means they were brought right across the Mediterranean and then sailed up the Guadalquivir.

Thanks to the columns, this road has been known as Calle de los Mármoles (Street of the Marbles) since at least the 15th century. A tile from Olavide's time (see p. 100) refers to it as Calle del Mármol.

NEARBY
The statues of Hercules and Julius Caesar
Alameda de Hércules

The two columns that were relocated to adorn the Alameda de Hércules were crowned by stone effigies of the mythical founders of the city: Hercules, who gave his name to the garden square and, according to legend, was the inspiration behind the location of the settlement; and Julius Caesar, who built the walls that protected it when he was quaestor of the province from 68 to 65 BCE and who gave the colony its name, *Julia Romula Hispalis*. Both statues were the work of sculptor Diego de Pesquera, who based his Hercules on Emperor Charles V and his Julius Caesar on Philip II.

HEAD OF KING PETER I

The monarch who sentenced himself to death

Calle Cabeza del Rey Don Pedro, 30

At No. 30 on the street that bears his name, a niche houses a bust of King Peter I (1334–69). The statue commemorates the story of a monarch who sentenced himself to death. According to legend, on one of his nocturnal escapades, Peter encountered a member of the Count de Niebla's Guzmán family – an ally of the House of Trastámara and therefore a sworn enemy – and killed him in this dark alley. On hearing the commotion, an elderly woman who lived nearby peered out of her window with an oil lamp and recognised the king. By royal decree, the death of a nobleman demanded that the killer be decapitated and his head put on public display at the scene of the crime. When the old woman was summoned as a witness to a private hearing, she nervously pointed to her sovereign. The guilty party's death sentence was passed in secret and orders were given for the head to be placed in a wooden casket – it was never to be opened, on pain of death. But the secret was soon out. In 1369, eight years after these events, Peter I was killed by his bastard brother Henry, who succeeded him as King of Castile. Once decapitated, Peter's head was stuck on the end of a lance and paraded around the cities that were still loyal to him. His body later ended up resting in the Capilla Real (Royal Chapel) of Seville Cathedral.

The first thing the Guzmán family did after the king's death was to open up the casket to discover the identity of the killer. They were astonished to find the box contained a stone bust of the king. To shame Peter in public, it was decided that the effigy would be exhibited for posterity.

To see the original bust, you need to visit the patio of the stables in Casa de Pilatos (see p. 116), which Fernando Enríquez de Ribera purchased in 1590 when the house where the statue used to stand was demolished. In 1630 sculptor Marcos Cabrera was commissioned to make the statue that now stands in Calle Cabeza del Rey Don Pedro, with crown, royal sceptre and hand on his sword.

The naming of the two streets Calle Cabeza del Rey Don Pedro and Calle Candilejo (from where the old lady looked out, with her oil lamp) means that both history and myth live on to this day.

Peter I of Castile was known alternately as either The Cruel or The Just. This depended on whether the speaker was friend or foe within the context of the fratricidal war with Henry of Trastámara, his Seville-born bastard brother. He was an important king in the history of the city, leaving such iconic buildings as the Real Alcázar (Royal Alcázar). A defender of the Jewish community, he reorganised the justice system and encouraged agriculture and livestock farming.

TORRE DE LOS DESCALZOS

A hidden bell tower reminiscent of a Russian Orthodox church

Calle Descalzos, 3

Scanning the neighbouring rooftops from the corner of Plaza del Cristo de Burgos that leads on to Calle Descalzos, you'll see a curious bell tower rising up, reminiscent of a Russian Orthodox church.

This tower, perhaps the most obscure of its kind in the city, was part of the old church belonging to the monastery of the Trinitarios Descalzos (Discalced Trinitarians), built in 1625 to a design by Juan de Segarra and devoted to La Virgen de Gracia (Our Lady of Grace). This great monastery, destroyed in the 19th century, was located between Calle Dormitorio and Calle Descalzos.

As regards the origins of this odd bulbous dome, decorated with brilliant cobalt-blue tiles, legend has it that a lay brother of Russian origin, nostalgic for the churches of his distant homeland, was responsible for its construction in the 18th century. This sort of dome was extremely common in the Byzantine architecture that spread mainly throughout Russia and Germany. Its form is sometimes considered a nod to the church of the Holy Sepulchre in Jerusalem, as well as symbolising the flames of burning candles. It is also known as the 'chess tower', doubtless on account of the little spires that look rather like pawns or bishops in chess.

Following the monastery's disentailment in 1836, the façade was knocked down and part of the building was converted into housing. During the French occupation, some magnificent Murillo paintings disappeared: their whereabouts are still unknown. The church continued to be used for worship until the 1868 Revolution, when the City Council gave the building to the Club Popular del Café de Emperadores. At the end of the 20th century, the bell tower was restored by the City Council and the building purchased by the Brotherhood of Santísimo Cristo de Burgos. All that's now left of the monastery is the tower, which is not open to the public.

Initials of the four main city gateways

According to legend, the prior of the monastery decided to install a tiled hieroglyph with the letters M, J, C and T on the four sides of the tower.

It seems that this hieroglyph, which isn't currently visible (nobody knows what happened to it), didn't refer to a verse from the Bible, but stood for the four main gateways of the city: Macarena, Jerez, Carmona and Triana. Like a bizarre wind rose guiding residents through the neighbourhood's labyrinthine streets.

PILA DEL PATO

The nomadic fountain

Plaza de San Leandro

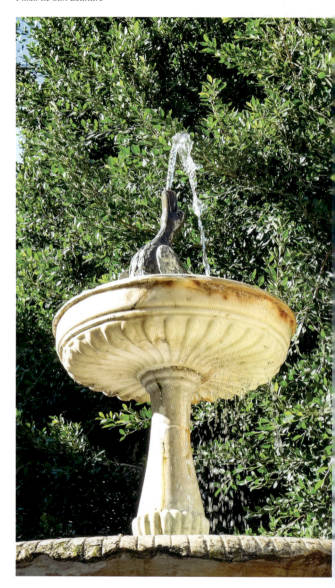

In a peaceful square opposite the convent of San Leandro, in the shade of one of the oldest trees in Seville, a fountain with one of the longest histories in the city lies at rest. And we say 'at rest' because this marble fountain has hardly stopped moving around for the past two centuries.

The Pila del Pato (Duck's Basin), whose authorship is unknown, consists of a reservoir of water out of which a baluster rises up, supporting two round basins, one above the other, adorned with animal forms and Renaissance decorations. The ensemble is crowned with a bronze duck, from where it gets its name.

The story began in 1833, when a fountain was commissioned to replace the one dedicated to Mercury in Plaza de San Francisco. It was cast by the Renaissance master Bartolomé Morel, also responsible for the weathervane that crowns the Giralda, the famous Giraldillo. Its place was taken by the Pila del Pato, which was then moved to a different location in the square so as not to obstruct the increasing volume of traffic.

Its stay there was brief, however, and in 1885 the fountain had to migrate to the Alameda de Hércules, very close to the columns with the lions. Local residents made it their own and the streets came alive with stories of the magical properties of the water that spurted out of it. It apparently bestowed good fortune on bullfighters seeking fame.

The fountain held out there until 1953, when it was moved to the area around the Prado de San Sebastián, near the old bus station. This was where the Feria de Abril (April Fair) was held, and the Pila del Pato soon became the place where locals would arrange to meet. In the words of one of the most famous singers of *sevillanas* of the day, Francisco Palacio (El Pali): 'At the Pila del Pato I met you, my love.'

Destiny had one more surprise in store for the fountain, meaning it had to move yet again. The expansion of the courthouses and the need for more parking space led to it being taken down yet again and sent to Plaza de las Mercedarias, before finding its final (for now, at least) resting place in Plaza de San Leandro.

GOBLIN'S GUARD STONE

The impish guardian of the house

Corner of Calle Imperial and Ensenada

O n the first stretch of Calle Imperial from the Plaza de San Leandro end, a metal plate protects the corner of the building with a relief featuring the impish, smiling face of a *duende* (meaning goblin, imp or sprite) under which is written: Fundición de Hierro de E. Balbontín (E. Balbontín Iron Foundry).

When carriages became a popular means of transporting passengers or merchandise across cities, the corners of buildings needed protecting, especially those located on the busier and narrower streets. It wasn't unusual for houses to be damaged by the continuous scraping of wheels, and even people were sometimes injured.

Over the years, these guard stones – also known as jostle stones or *chasse-roues* (wheel catchers) – have taken on all sorts of forms. They often recycle unwanted materials, which may over time even become archaeological reference points.

As such, you can find marble columns from all periods (such as the one preserved in Casa de la Moneda, see p. 225) or bronze cannons pointing downwards. In other towns and cities, Roman milestones or train or tram rails have been used. On the doorways of important houses where carriages used to roll up, these *chasse-roues* may be in stone, marble or metal. Noble Seville houses frequently used huge millstones (see p. 178) to protect the walls from the wear and tear caused by carriage wheel shafts.

Metal imps are found on other corners across the city: for example, on Calle Jimios, Calle Harinas and Calle Duende (a name dating back to at least 1784).

Founded in 1864, the Balbontín, Orta y Cía company specialised in the manufacture of agricultural machinery. Its headquarters was in the Calle Goles area, near both the river and the railway, like many other Seville foundries.

CORRAL DEL CONDE

A hidden urban oasis

Calle Santiago, 27
Wednesday 10am–2pm
Admission free
The concierge does not usually allow visitors at other times

Occupying a large plot with its outer walls overlooking Calle Santiago, Calle Ave María and Calle Azafrán, the Corral del Conde (*Corral* of the Count) is one of the last vestiges of a particular type of working-class architecture, perhaps the grandest and most interesting of all.

Due to its L-shape and wooden balconies in the style of old-fashioned *corrales de comedias* (open-air theatres), it can be dated to the

18th century, though there are traces of its Islamic origins, as is the case with similar buildings throughout the city.

In much the same way as in Moorish houses, there is a side rather than a direct entrance, with a tight bend and just one door, thereby ensuring security and protecting residents from outside ... a hidden urban oasis.

The patio was the central social and shared living space, as well as providing the communal services lacking in these modest households: a fountain or well, kitchens, washrooms, clothes lines, latrines ... and even a bread oven and a little chapel that still survives today.

These tenement blocks, whose emergence played a major part in the history of Seville, were arranged around one or more inner patios. They were either purpose-built or converted from mansions, palaces or old convents.

In 1983 this *corral* was in a deplorable state and needed painstaking renovation – it was converted into apartments. In the early 20th century, it would have housed around 120 families, generally of modest means, who often rented the little units (with a maximum of two rooms) along passageways at various levels. It was home to carpenters, builders, cigarette sellers, blacksmiths, carters, washerwomen, clothes pressers, seamstresses, maids, shoemakers, machine operators from the artillery or gunshot factory (see p. 40) and a host of other trades. And of course there was the landlady, representing the owner, who was in charge of collecting the rent, organising shared tasks, resolving disputes between neighbours and even evicting insolvent or problematic tenants.

The *corral* still conjures up the ruckus of children playing, the chit-chat of neighbours on summer evenings, occasional heated arguments, the festivities of a christening, dancing the *sevillana* for the Cruz de Mayo (Cross of May) celebrations or the wails and commiserations at the funeral wake of a resident. Echoes of a city life long gone ...

WEATHERVANE OF ST JAMES THE MOOR-SLAYER

27

The legend of the warrior apostle

Church of Santiago
Calle Santiago, 31
Monday & Thursday 11am–1pm & 6pm–9pm, Sunday 11.30am–1pm

Under the cross of the Order of Santiago, the cast-iron weathervane crowning the bell gable of the church of Santiago shows the apostle on horseback attacking a Moorish soldier with his spear. The building over which it presides was originally one of the churches established by Ferdinand III in the 13th century after the conquest of Seville. This meant converting a mosque for Christian worship – in this case, dedicated to the apostle who had evangelised Spain, according to a medieval legend.

According to this legend, St James the Moor-slayer (known in Spanish as Santiago Matamoros) appeared to King Ramiro I of Asturias, saying that he would be joining his troops in the fight against the forces of Abd al-Rahman II to prevent delivery of the annual tribute of 100 young Christian virgins. This apparition was identified as the reason behind the Christian victory in the mythical battle of Clavijo (Rioja region) in 844, where some people even believed they saw the warrior apostle on a white steed, brandishing a sword.

In addition to the weathervane, this story is illustrated in a large-scale painting by the Italian Matteo Pérez de Alesio (or da Leccia) found at the bottom of the nave on the Epistle side of the church of Santiago.

The Order of Santiago emerged in the 12th century, adopting a red Cross in the form of a sword as its emblem, recalling the myth of the warrior saint. This order, which was originally created for the protection of pilgrims on the Camino de Santiago (Way of St James), played a major role in the conquest of Seville.

Jacobean way

We know that James the Great, one of Christ's first disciples, was sentenced to be beheaded by order of the King of Judea, Herod Agrippa I, at some point between 41 and 44 CE. According to the somewhat convoluted myth behind the origin of the Camino de Santiago, after his death the apostle was disinterred by his followers and sent off on a stone boat on a miraculous journey from Palestine to Galicia.

Almost 800 years later, in around 813, the Galician bishop Theodemir found a body in a possibly Roman cemetery with its head under its arm, which he identified as being the remains of the apostle. This gave rise to the third most important Christian pilgrimage in the world, after Jerusalem and Rome – according to some, a Christianisation of the old *Vía del Finisterre*, the route followed by Celtic tribes to the supposed end of the world.

28

ST PETER'S ROOSTER

The ashes of the rooster that crowed on the night that Peter thrice denied Christ?

Casa de Pilatos
Plaza de Pilatos, 1
954 22 52 98
fundacionmedinaceli.org/monumentos/pilatos
Daily, November–March 9am–6pm; April–October 9am–7pm
Admission free: Monday 3pm–7pm

The magnificent Casa de Pilatos (House of Pilate), offers an array of artistic and historical objects of interest, with no shortage of secrets or unusual items. One of these is a curious oil-painted panel featuring a rooster locked behind an iron grille framed in a wall of Renaissance tiles on the stairs going up to the first floor.

According to legend, the panel conceals an urn with the ashes of the rooster that crowed on the night that Peter denied Christ three times. This was one of the relics that the owner of the palace, Fadrique Enríquez de Ribera, Marquis de Tarifa, brought back after his pilgrimage to Jerusalem in the 16th century.

Born to two of the most important noble families in Andalusia, Fadrique Enríquez joined his father in the conquest of Granada, where he was an armed knight at the age of 16. As an older man, he decided to undertake a pilgrimage to the holy sites where the Passion and death of Jesus took place in order to attain the promised indulgences. The trip lasted almost two years: he set out from Bornos (Cádiz) in 1518 and finally returned to Seville in 1520. His entourage consisted of his major-domo, a chaplain and eight servants, and his itinerary took in Valencia, Marseille, Milan and Venice, from where they set sail for Rhodes and Cyprus, finally docking at the port of Jaffa.

His experience provided the material for his *Viaje a Jerusalén* (Journey to Jerusalem), published in 1521 by the Casa de Pilatos' own press, an authentic guide for future pilgrims, where he recorded everything he saw and that happened to him. After arriving in the Holy Land, then under Turkish rule, the Muslims charged him for everything you can imagine. The excited pilgrim was shown around incredible and dilapidated sites: the site where Pontius Pilate washed his hands, the place where the lamb for the Last Supper was roasted, a rock with Christ's fingerprints, the hole in the beam of the Cross ... and he was offered all sorts of relics, from nails to pieces of the Cross and the bones of saints ... and (who knows?) perhaps an urn containing the ashes of the famous cockerel.

The book mentions one of the places he was shown by the Moors (and for which honour he had to pay an ungodly sum): it was the supposed house of the high priest Caiaphas, 'where they say the fire was, where St Peter denied Christ ... and a little window by the door, where they say the rooster was.'

MASONIC SYMBOLS IN THE CHURCH OF SAN ESTEBAN

Compasses and Ruler, Square and Gavel

Calle San Esteban, 1
Tuesday & Thursday 6pm–8.30pm

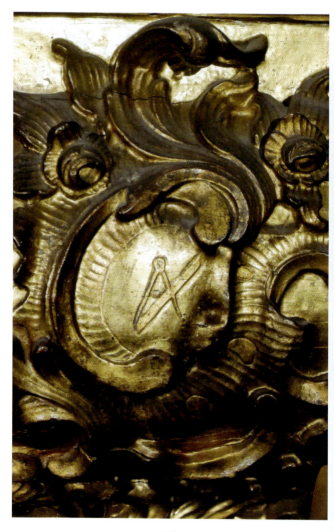

In the secluded sacramental chapel of the church of San Esteban, an enigmatic secret is hidden in clear sight for any visitor. Look closely at the 17th-century gilt Baroque altarpiece presided over by Our Lady of the Immaculate Conception: at the foot of the columns on each side, symbols of obviously Masonic origin are engraved in the wood. At the bottom of the right-hand column, in the middle of a circle made up of wooden volutes, the crossed symbols of the *Compasses* and *Ruler* can be made out, while the left-hand column has a crossed *Square* and *Gavel*.

Independently, these symbols could be linked to Freemasonry as a possible identification mark for the unknown artisan who made the altarpiece. Appearing as they do in crossed pairs, however, is a far more direct reference, given that they could be associated with the rise from Apprentice level to that of Fellowcraft.

These are some of the most significant symbols in the Freemasons' language of architectural metaphor and are marks used by the builders of cathedrals.

The first pair of symbols consists of the *Compasses* that symbolise perfection (where the points of the circumference stand for mankind, and the centre is the Mason who should bear the light of truth and the benefits of science) and the *Ruler* (a symbol of rectitude in the compliance of moral duty and ethics, as well as moderation and temperance). The second pair consists of the *Gavel*, which symbolises constancy, resistance and will, and the *Square*, which represents order and the limits that should constrain human actions. Each tool has its own symbolism referring to the values by which Masons should live their daily lives.

Church of San Esteban

The church of San Esteban was one of the first to be founded in Seville following the Christian conquest. It was originally established on the site of a mosque and its most important transformations were both due to earthquakes – the first leading to its reconstruction in the 14th century as a Gothic-Mudéjar church and, later, in 1755, its conversion into a Baroque church. Of particular note are the seven paintings by Zurbarán in the presbytery, which also boasts a magnificent brick altar table, whose frontal features 14th-century Mudéjar *alicatado* tiling, discovered during restoration work in the main chapel.

CANNON SHELL OF THE ANDALUSIAN CANTON

Puerta de Carmona barricades

Corner of Calle Mosqueta and Calle San Esteban

At the intersection of Calle Mosqueta and Calle San Esteban you can see a cannon shell lodged in the wall, as if in a little religious niche. This piece of ammunition was found by the owner of the house when it was renovated in the 1980s, buried in the wall just where the Puerta de Carmona would have been.

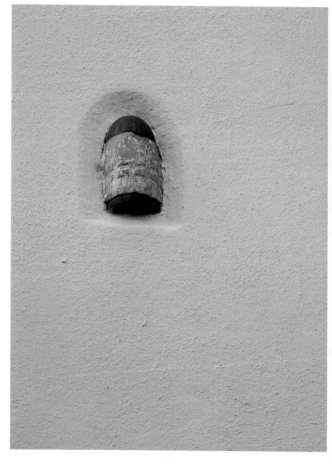

Apparently, the cannon shell came from General Manuel Pavía's bombardment of Seville's Andalusian Cantonal uprising in the late 19th century – their strongest line of defence was in the San Bartolomé neighbourhood between the Carne and Carmona gateways. The barricades were erected right here by the locals and by Republican volunteers with their red caps and esparto-grass espadrilles.

The cannon shell is cylindrical/conical, oblong and has grooves, an innovation adopted by the Spanish artillery in 1858 to give increased accuracy and range. As all shells prior to that point had been round, this sort of missile came to be known by the colloquial nickname *pepino* (cucumber) or *pepinazo* (big cucumber), an expression that lives on today.

Brief history of the Seville Canton

The Cantonal Rebellion broke out in Spain in June 1873, mainly in Andalusia and the eastern Levante region, following the declaration of the First Republic. The Canton was proclaimed as a demand for greater administrative decentralisation, and social reforms such as an eight-hour working day and the right to work. In response, the central government sent General Pavía with his troops on two trains from Madrid. For two days Seville witnessed a bloody confrontation which saw the deaths of 300 soldiers and many more volunteers from the Cantonal side. On 1 August Pavía made his triumphal entrance into the city, thereby putting an end to the Seville Cantonal experience. The next day he went on to attack Jerez and Cádiz.

Puerta de Carmona

Until it was demolished in 1870, the imposing Puerta de Carmona stood at what is now the intersection of Calle Mosqueta and Calle San Esteban. This was one of the most important gateways for merchandise and people entering the city, even boasting a turret to one side with a prison for knights. It was also the site of the end of the aqueduct to which it gave its name, the Caños de Carmona (see p. 128).

MONUMENT TO ANTONIO MACHÍN ㉛

The only mixed-race member of the 'Brotherhood of dark brothers'

Plaza de Carmen Benítez

Despite the presence of Guillermo Plaza's sculpture of Antonio Machín playing the maracas while looking ironically at the chapel of Los Negritos, many people are still unaware of the link between this extraordinary Cuban singer and Seville.

A renowned figure from the *bolero* and *son Cubano* traditions, Machín became famous for his song *El manisero*, leading to tours of the US and Europe. He was performing in Paris when the Second World War broke out in 1939 but he fled the Nazis and headed to Barcelona, where he faced the harsh realities of the post-Civil-War regime. He subsequently ended up in Seville, where his brother Juan Gualberto lived, having worked as a plumber at several pavilions at the 1929 Expo – he was the only mixed-race member on the committee of the Los Negritos Brotherhood in the 20th century.

Founded in the 14th century, this brotherhood was the oldest in Seville. In its earliest days, its members included both blacks and people of mixed race, whether free men or slaves, and was known as 'the Brotherhood of Our Lady of the Angels, who is Our Lady of the dark brothers'.

Machín 'didn't need to sing to eat, but to live'

Antonio Machín was born in February 1903 to a poor and numerous family in Sagua la Grande (Cuba). He became a musician at a tender age, being the first black singer to perform in Havana's exclusive Casino Nacional. From that moment on, he never stopped singing – whether in Cuba or abroad – as part of such legendary ensembles as the Azpiazu and Habana orchestras, the Machín quartet and so on. He had an endless succession of hits, including *Perfidia*, *Mira que eres linda*, *Envidia*, *Camarera de mi amor* and *Dos gardenias* ... and, of course, the anti-racist bolero entitled *Angelitos negros*, which catapulted him to stardom.

In Christmas 1941 he made his debut performance in Seville, where he met his wife Angelita Rodríguez, a young woman from Córdoba who lived on Pasaje Mallol. They married in the church of San Luis de los Franceses and lived in the street that now bears his name. His last performance, just two months before his death and when he was already suffering from a severe lung complaint, took place in Alcalá de Guadaíra. He died at 74 and was buried in Seville cemetery on the express wishes of the man who 'didn't need to sing to eat, but to live'.

Each year, on the anniversary of his death (4 August), some admirer will emulate the sound of his voice and decorate his final resting place with gardenias and Cuban rum, under the watchful eye of the black marble angel that stands over his tomb.

MASONIC SYMBOLS IN DR SERAS' LABORATORY

The pentagram and the sprig of acacia

Avenida Luis Montoto, 7

A t the beginning of Avenida Luis Montoto, the façade of Dr Seras' laboratory has an interesting series of elements linked to Freemasonry. Like many late-19th- and early-20th-century professionals

and intellectuals, Antonio de Seras became a Mason. He was a member of the Isis y Osiris lodge, the most influential of the three that existed in the city, whose temple was on what is now Calle Lirio, on the ground floor of the house of Diego Martínez Barrio, who served as President of the Second Spanish Republic.

It was in this lodge in 1934 that de Seras attained the degree of Fellowcraft, taking on the symbolic name of *Guillermo Tell* (William Tell). After the Civil War, he escaped the firing squad because his family were acquaintances of General Queipo de Llano, but he was disbarred from practising medicine and harassed in his final years, as well as being forced to resign as chairman of the College of Veterinarians.

The front façade features three areas, each with three windows (this is the most highly symbolic number in Freemasonry, with a huge range of significances, from the three degrees of Masons: Apprentice, Fellowcraft and Master; to the three pillars on which the lodge is built: wisdom, strength and beauty). Crowning each of these groups of windows is a relief that incorporates two important elements from Masonic aesthetics: the sprig of acacia (see below) and the five-pointed star or pentagram (see double-page spread overleaf).

The building, designed by architect Simón Barris y Bes in 1905, is the city's foremost example of modernism; the upper section has a relief dedicated to Louis Pasteur. The doctor and veterinarian Antonio de Seras y González (1871–1941) had previously worked at the Pasteur Institute in Paris and he commissioned this building as the Provincial Hygiene Institute. It was here that he became one of the benchmark figures in Spanish bacteriology, developing key vaccines for smallpox and the bubonic plague, and treatments for syphilis.

Acacia: a Masonic symbol of immortality

The sprig of acacia is one of the symbols of the Masonic degree of Master and symbolises immortality, innocence and the domination of the human spirit over nature.

In Hebrew culture, the acacia is mentioned as early as the Old Testament, being used for the construction of the most holy objects (Ark, Table and Altar) due to its ability to resist decay.

Its name comes from the Greek word *akis*, which means point or barb, precisely because of the acacia's thorns. These represent the obstacles and painful trials that initiates must tackle and overcome on the path leading to the degree of Master.

Symbolism of the pentagram, the five-pointed star

The pentagram is a five-pointed star made up of five straight lines. It was originally the symbol of the Roman goddess Venus, and as such was associated with that planet due to its orbit, which, seen from Earth and according to Ptolemaic astronomy, seems to trace out a five-pointed star every eight years.

In nature, the sign of the fifth element (or quintessence), Ether, occupies the upper point of the pentagram, while the other four elements (Air, Fire, Water and Earth) occupy the lower points.

The pentagram (or *pentalfa*) is also a symbol of the Infinite; in the pentagon at the centre of the pentagram, another smaller pentagram can be created, and so on ad infinitum.

It possesses multiple symbolic meanings, always based on the number 5, which represents a union between the masculine (3) and the feminine (2), thereby symbolically bringing opposites together, a requisite of spiritual enlightenment.

As such, in Pythagorean mathematics, the pentagram (symbol of that Greek institution) is related to the *golden ratio* (1.618): in a pentagram, which is made up of a regular pentagon and five isosceles triangles, the ratio between the sides of the triangles and the base (the side of the pentagon) is equal to the *golden ratio*.

Through its most learned rabbis, the Jewish Kabbalah holds that the pentagram is the symbol of the will of God and divine protection.

In Christianity, it is the Christmas star, that of Christ's birth, which heralds the Resurrection, both of spirit in body (birth) and body in spirit (resurrection).

In Freemasonry, it is the flaming star of initiation, placed on the eastern side of the lodge. It also symbolises resurrection, following the death of the profane, which is converted into a new adept.

The inverted pentagram is generally associated with Evil, as opposed to Good, repre- sented by the upright (starred) pentagram. This means that the Spirit has been plunged into the blindness of Matter and the carnal sufferings of the human spirit.

CAÑOS DE CARMONA

33

Remains of the great Almohad aqueduct

Avenida Luis Montoto, 19 and 23

Only three sections remain from the great aqueduct that used to provide Seville's main water supply. Of these, the two that are closest to the city centre are at the start of Avenida Luis Montoto. Both are built from brick, though the first section is only one arch high while the second has two rows of arches on top of each other for a length of five arches. A Corten steel portico was added when the aqueduct was renovated in 2009, making an interesting contrast with the Almohad brickwork.

The section of aqueduct furthest out from the centre, and perhaps the least well known of the three, is to be found outside No. 10 Calle Cigüeña, in the Pajaritos district.

This feat of hydraulic engineering – unique in Spain – dates back to the Almohad period, making use of an earlier channel of Roman origin. It was inaugurated in 1172 by Caliph Abu Yaqub Yusuf, who was also responsible for building the Great Mosque and its towering minaret (today's Giralda), the floating or pontoon bridge across the Guadalquivir and the palace and gardens of La Buhaira (see p. 192).

The aqueduct was popularly known as the Caños de Carmona (Pipes of Carmona), not because it started there, but because the final reservoir from which the water was distributed was near the gateway of that name. In fact, it started its journey in Alcalá de Guadaíra, in the Santa Lucía spring, then going underground (its longest stretch) towards Torreblanca. From there it continued to the Pajaritos district along an open channel, also used for irrigating agricultural plots and even operating flour mills. Finally, it terminated at the Puerta de Carmona, with an elevated section 1,200 metres long boasting 400 semicircular arches, in some places including an upper row. The water was carried for a total of 17.2 km. The height of the aqueduct enabled it to supply water to practically the entire walled section of the city, with enough of an incline to reach the San Vicente district. The capacity was 5,000 cubic metres: once the top-quality drinking water had reached the city, it was divided between the Alcázar on the one hand and the remaining districts on the other.

From the 12th to the 19th centuries its physical appearance was unchanged, though it underwent continuous repairs and renovations. In 1912, despite vociferous opposition, it was demolished on the orders of the City Council – leaving only the three stretches seen today.

CRUZ DEL CAMPO

34

A Gothic Calvary surrounded by modern buildings

Calle Luis Montoto, 143

One question that springs to mind when you come across this magnificent little Gothic-Mudéjar monumental crucifix at the end of Calle Luis Montoto, itself quite a trek from the city centre: just where is the *campo* (countryside) to which it refers? Because it seems uncomfortably penned in by the mediocre urban development that has sprung up around it.

If you look carefully at the dome, you'll see some paintings that were revealed during recent restoration work. Gothic characters mark the year 1482, the date when Seville's *asistente mayor* (city mayor or governor), Diego de Merlo, commissioned the Calvary, during the reign of the Catholic Monarchs and right in the middle of the war with the Kingdom of Granada. Merlo, who would die that same year, was also behind the restoration of the nearby Caños de Carmona aqueduct (see p. 128).

The Calvary houses a white marble Cross featuring an image of the Virgin on one side and a Crucified Christ on the other. Erected in the second half of the 16th century, the Cross is attributed to Juan Bautista Vázquez the Elder. Also known as the Ermita del Humilladero (chapel of the Calvary), it was located outside the city walls on one of the city's main thoroughfares, with the aqueduct passing close by. Wayside crosses were used at intersections to mark borders with neighbouring towns and were also a reminder for travellers to kneel in an act of humility, from which the Spanish word for this sort of monumental Cross, '*humilladero*', is derived.

Another Calvary apparently existed on the same spot at least as early as 1380, with a modest wooden Cross near the since-disappeared Hospital de Los Negros, whose chapel was the headquarters of the Brotherhood of Los Santos Ángeles. This brotherhood, the oldest in the city, and known today as Los Negritos (see p. 122), allowed free black men to be members, along with slaves who had obtained written permission from their masters.

Following his pilgrimage to the Holy Land in the 16th century (see p. 116), Fadrique Enríquez de Ribera, the Marquis de Tarifa, introduced the custom of undertaking a Via Crucis in the city. The first of its 12 stages was at his residence, known from that point on as Casa de Pilatos (House of Pilate), and the last stage finished at the Cruz del Campo *humilladero*, Seville's very own Golgotha, thereby marking the origin of the modern Holy Week celebrations.

Since 1904 the Calvary has been the image of the city's premium lager, Cruzcampo, whose factory is located nearby. After years of neglect, and thanks to the owner of the brand, the Calvary was restored in 2008.

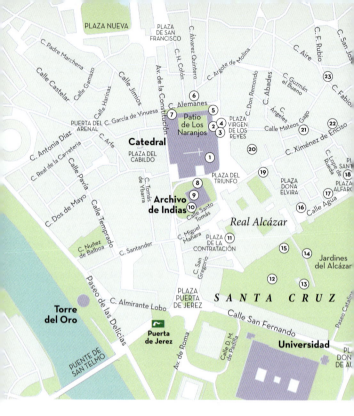

Santa Cruz, Cathedral
and San Bartolomé

SECRET DOOR TO CHRISTOPHER COLUMBUS'S TOMB

The travelling remains of the discoverer

Seville Cathedral – Plaza del Triunfo
catedraldesevilla.com
Monday 10.30am–4pm, Tuesday–Saturday 10.30am–6pm, Sunday 2pm–7pm
Admission free: Monday 4.30pm–6pm

In the nave on the epistle side of Seville Cathedral, just opposite the San Cristóbal entrance, there is an impressive funerary monument executed by Arturo Mélida in 1891. On the left-hand side is the coat of arms the Catholic Monarchs granted Columbus in 1493, which

conceals a secret compartment.

The upper field of the shield features the royal arms of Castile and Leon, while the lower section is taken up by those granted to the admiral of the Oceanic Seas: a group of islands in gold to represent the lands discovered, and five anchors.

Look closely and you'll see three keyholes hidden in the shield: on the castle gate, one of the islands and in the eyelet of one of the anchors.

The keys to these three keyholes (one of which is in the possession of Columbus's descendants, the Ducal House of Veragua) open a trapdoor that leads onto a little chamber containing a gilt lead casket holding the bones of the explorer. But are they really his remains?

The story surrounding the tomb of Christopher Columbus is very much a reflection of how his life was. If he lived a continuous toing and froing from one sea to another, from one court to another and, finally, from one continent to another, his tomb has matched him, pace for pace.

Columbus died in Valladolid in 1506, where he was buried until three years later when his remains were moved to the Cartuja monastery in Seville. At some unspecified time, well into the 16th century, his remains moved on to the cathedral of Santo Domingo, constituting his fifth crossing of the Atlantic. There they rested until 1795, the year Spain lost control of Hispaniola (today's Haiti and the Dominican Republic), which led to his remains setting sail once more, this time heading for the cathedral of Havana. The final journey made by the discoverer's remains took place with the loss of Cuba in 1898; the mausoleum awaiting him in Seville cathedral was his destination.

To mark the 500th anniversary of his death, the University of Granada undertook a complete analysis of all available DNA from near relations (brother and son), and concluded that the remains are indeed those of Christopher Columbus. After so many comings and goings, only a part of him returned; the contents of the urn weigh barely 150 g, which would account for 15 per cent of his entire skeleton.

LIZARD IN THE CATHEDRAL

Regal gifts, sumptuous fabrics, exquisite drugs and strange animals

Seville Cathedral
Plaza del Triunfo
catedraldesevilla.com
Monday 10.30am–4pm, Tuesday–Saturday 10.30am–6pm, Sunday 2pm–7pm
Admission free: Monday 4.30pm–6pm

The nave of the *lagarto* (lizard) is accessed via the Almohad doorway on the left-hand side of the Giralda entrance, and its curious name, recorded at least as early as 1349, becomes clear if you look up and observe the great crocodile, popularly known as the *lagarto*, hanging from the ceiling. There are also a number of other strange items hanging from the horseshoe arch next to it, including an ivory tusk, a bridle and a wooden cane. According to the chronicles of the day, on 30 May 1261 the city welcomed a lavish envoy sent by Baibars I, the Sultan of Egypt and Syria, to mark the celebration of the anniversary of the death of Ferdinand III. The solemn ambassadorial entourage, which brought 'regal gifts, sumptuous fabrics, exquisite drugs and strange animals' was seeking the friendship of Ferdinand's son, Alfonso X.

The animals accompanying the messengers included an enormous Egyptian crocodile, a trained giraffe with saddle and bridle, and 'an ass with white and black stripes' (a zebra). It appears they were taken to the Real Alcázar, which became a garden of wild animals, though they did not survive the extreme and changeable Seville climate for long. The king ordered their skins to be stuffed with straw and put on display in the cloisters of the great church, with the giant lizard from

the Nile being the one that resisted the longest, hanging from the ceiling. In the 16th century the battered remains of the crocodile were replaced by a wooden carving painted green. A century later, when it was taken down to be cleaned, a piece of paper was shoved into its mouth, giving an account of its story.

Many Christian churches contain stuffed animals, whale bones and so on. The closest example would be the alligator in the chapel of Consolación in Utrera, just 20 km away. Another alligator brought from the Americas is to be found on the wall of the church of Fuensanta in Córdoba. The most obvious symbolism links them to hell, where their open mouths stand for the gates of the abyss. Other interpretations associate lizards with wisdom or relate them to an allegory of silence in holy places.

GIRALDA CLOCK CHAMBER

Marking time in Seville for centuries

Seville Cathedral
Plaza del Triunfo
catedraldesevilla.com
Monday 10.30am–4pm, Tuesday–Saturday 10.30am–6pm,
Sunday 2pm–7pm
Admission free: Monday 4.30pm–6pm

As you pass through the entrance arch to the tower of the Giralda, you start up the 35 ramps that lead to the bell tower. And it was

up the ramps of the 12th-century Almohad mosque's majestic minaret that the muezzin would ride on horseback five times a day to call the faithful to prayer.

There are seven vaulted chambers concealed inside the tower, one of which may be accessed each five sections of ramp, though visitors tend not to pay them much attention, intent on reaching the vantage point at the top.

These rooms were used by the tower's servants, probably the muezzins first and, in all likelihood, the bell ringers afterwards. Both had the same objective: to mark the hour of prayer for the city's faithful.

Ramp No. 25 is where the clock chamber is to be found, housing the Giralda timepiece manufactured by the Franciscan monk José Cordero in 1764. This was the fruit of seven years of work, commissioned to replace the old clock that was installed on 20 June 1400 in the presence of King Henry III, becoming one of the first public clocks in Spain.

On the clock face you can make out the name of its maker and the word *español*, to emphasize the nationality of the authorship of the complex clockwork machinery that remained active for two centuries, until the 1960s.

Alonso Domínquez's chiming bell from the 15th-century clock has survived, known as 'San Miguel de las Victorias'. It remains in the body of the clock towards the top of the Giralda, above the belfry.

Ten minutes slow

Brother José Cordero's clock lagged 10 minutes behind the official time in Spain because it was set to the city's solar time rather than the Greenwich meridian. Popular myth had it this delay was in the interest of prisoners sentenced to death, giving them a few extra minutes to wait for a royal pardon.

The second chamber houses the authentic bronze knockers from the cathedral's Puerta del Perdón entrance; the third features a stone plaque commemorating one of the knights who conquered Seville, Catalan Petrús de la Cera; the fourth is dedicated to the machines used to build the cathedral.

Daughter of the Giralda

Over the doorway to the seventh chamber there is a tile marking the birth of the daughter of the second bell ringer. Later known as the 'daughter of the Giralda', Sister Bárbara de Santo Domingo was famous for her mystical visions.

ROMAN STELES
IN THE GIRALDA

Commemorative marble slabs reused in building the minaret

Torre de la Giralda
Plaza Virgen de los Reyes

One of the secrets of the Giralda tower is clearly visible to any curious passers-by: two Roman steles with Latin inscriptions at the foot of the majestic minaret.

It was extremely common in Moorish architecture to reuse Roman or Visigothic materials, like these marble slabs the builders laid at the four corners of the tower to stabilise it.

These blocks of marble, which are often confused with funeral headstones, are actually commemorative steles, erected in the second half of the 2nd century CE by the corporation of Seville sailors. They would originally have been placed close to the port area of the river.

The inscription on the first of the steles refers to the gratitude of the city's boatmen to Sextus Julius, a prominent figure and military leader, commander of the Cohort of the Gauls, the Syrian Archers and an Ala of the Hispanic Cavalry, as well as being in charge of the African and Spanish oil trade.

The second stele is dedicated (once again by the local boatmen) to Lucius Castritius, son of Quintus Honoratus.

Recent archaeological work on the Giralda's foundations has also revealed a range of Roman pieces relating to olive-oil producers.

All of these marble works bear witness to the importance of the city's port, geared towards the exportation of products such as oil, wine, cereals and minerals to the entire empire.

Bear in mind that Rome is home to Monte Testaccio, an artificial hill made up by the accumulation of old oil amphorae (over 53 million broken amphorae!), more than 80 per cent of which contained Andalusian oil.

Almohad minaret

The new great mosque was built towards the end of the 12th century. An astonishing feat of architecture crowned by the tower of the minaret, which at 82 metres was the tallest tower in Europe in the Middle Ages. Following the Christian conquest the mosque was pulled down, but the tower and ritual ablutions and orange tree patios were preserved. The tower kept its spectacular *yamur*, the four enormous gilt bronze balls that crowned it, until they fell victim to an earthquake in 1356. It wasn't until the 16th century that the Giralda, the current bell tower, was built, with its 24 bells, and the enormous bronze weather vane (Giraldillo) was put on top, raising the total height of the tower to 101 metres.

BIBLIOTECA COLOMBINA

One of the most valuable Renaissance libraries

Calle Alemanes (no number)
954 56 07 69
biblioteca@icolombina.es – icolombina.es/colombina
Monday–Friday 9am–2pm, Monday & Tuesday 4.30pm–7.30pm (mornings only during the summer)
Free guided tours with prior booking

On the left of the cathedral's Puerta del Perdón entrance is the Library of Ferdinand Columbus, one of the most valuable Renaissance libraries, and an oddly little-known attraction.

Inside this splendid building, which is on the site of the great mosque's former ritual ablutions patio, is Christopher Columbus' tombstone, brought from Havana Cathedral along with his remains in 1899. A steep stairway through an old Moorish arch leads to a series of rooms lined by old oak bookshelves. The portrait of Ferdinand Columbus (1488–1539), Christopher's second son, presides over the main room, keeping close watch on the comings and goings of visitors and researchers.

One of the main display cabinets features a selection of works of incalculable value, arranged and stacked by the expert librarian employed to that end. Of particular note, having been owned by Christopher Columbus himself, are rare volumes including a 1480 copy of Cardinal Pierre d'Ailly's *Imago Mundi,* a volume of *The Travels of Marco Polo* from 1484, and a 1489 edition of Pliny the Elder's *Natural History,* fundamental works in the discovery of America project, with margin notes in his own hand. Not to mention his own unpublished manuscript, the *Book of Prophesies,* from which 14 of the original 84 folios have been ripped out.

The more interesting acquisitions by Ferdinand Columbus include a 1492 *Castilian Grammar* by Antonio de Nebrija and Erasmus of Rotterdam's *Antibarbarorum Liber,* dated 1520, a work that had been banned by the Inquisition and which includes an author's dedication. It's curious to see how in all his books Ferdinand wrote down the date and place he purchased them, and the price.

These works are just a small part of the 3,500 titles left to the cathedral by Ferdinand Columbus, and that have survived to this day, out of the vast collection of 15,350 volumes he acquired on his travels throughout Europe. Easy to imagine how, in the many years that have passed, a good number of these disappeared, due both to security failings and a lack of interest.

Note that in the 18th century the cathedral cleaners were left in charge of book maintenance, as they had the keys to the storage rooms and library. A far cry from the painstaking care with which this collection is currently being preserved, and which also includes the cathedral's enormous historical library, with its total of 70,000 volumes.

ARIAS CORREA'S PILLAR

In memory of a slave trader

Corner of Calle Alemanes and Calle Hernando Colón

Supporting a building on the corner of Calle Alemanes, just opposite the cathedral's Puerta del Perdón entrance, a pillar bears the inscription 'Arias Correa built this house in the year 1591'. It seems that Correa was a major slave trader who had his house built towards the end of the 16th century, of which only the pillars have survived. It stood opposite his place of work, on whose steps he traded in human beings; a despicable business that made him a wealthy man.

Site of the main slave market in 16th and 17th-century Seville

Calle Alemanes, for many years known as Calle de las Gradas, on account of the great steps (*gradas*) running alongside the cathedral, was home to Seville's main slave market during the 16th and 17th centuries. From the end of the 15th century Seville, along with Lisbon, was one of the cities with the greatest slave-trading activity. It was initially a hub for the importation of black Africans, and later that of Moors following the conquest of the Kingdom of Granada, along with slaves from the Canary Islands and the recently discovered West Indies. Many of these had their cheeks branded with an S with a nail going diagonally through it, representing the word 'slave', so all would know they were not free. It is estimated that at the end of the 16th century 7 per cent of Seville's huge population of 120,000 were slaves. This racial contrast led Cervantes to describe the population of Seville as being like a chessboard.

Owning slaves was a symbol of distinction for the social elites, the Church and also for many artisans and merchants. The majority of these worked in domestic service, but they could also be put to hard labour as farmers, builders, foundry workers, tanners, craftsmen, water sellers or transporting heavy loads on the dockside. Some even worked as nuns' servants.

Slaves in Seville art

Painters such as Velázquez and Murillo portrayed the presence of slaves in Seville society. Highlights are *The Kitchen Maid*, painted by Velázquez in 1620 (National Gallery, Dublin, see below), and the portrait of Juan de Pareja, dating from 1661, a slave of Morisco origin and the painter's assistant (Hispanic Society of America, New York). Murillo's *Three Boys*, from 1670, depicts a black water seller (Dulwich Picture Gallery, London).

HURRAHS IN THE CATHEDRAL

Ancient graffiti written in animal blood and plant pigments

Steps of Seville Cathedral
Corner of Calle Alemanes and Avenida de la Constitución

On the stretch of Calle Alemanes between the Puerta del Perdón and Avenida de la Constitución, letters, number and symbols can be seen written in red on the wall of the church of El Sagrario. And there are more on the wall at the corner, going round into Avenida de la Constitución. Their existence came to light thanks to painstaking

cleaning and preservation work undertaken in recent years, revealing graffiti written in animal blood and plant pigments that has survived the passing years. Dating from the 17th and 18th centuries, these were known as *vítores* or *víctores*, and were quite common in the university towns of the day, as outbursts of jubilation, a sort of 'hurrah', expressed by students who wished to leave written proof of having passed the exams that would shape their futures. Those that are perfectly legible include the *vítores* of Don Alonso García and Don Melchor, alongside others that can't be deciphered.

Medieval doors made from bronze and Atlas cedar

The main entrance to the Patio de los Naranjos (Patio of the Orange Trees) is recorded as early as 1196, when the Almohad Caliph Abu Yusuf ordered the esplanade to be enlarged. In fact, the Puerta del Perdón, so-called since at least 1363, is Seville Cathedral's oldest entrance. Incredibly, the enormous bronze-clad Atlas cedar doors have survived to this day, standing more than 7 metres tall and almost 2 metres wide. They date from the Almohad period, in the last decade of the 12th century. Their intricate geometric design is a repetition, in Kufic script, of the Koranic verses: 'All power belongs to Allah' and 'Eternity is Allah's' The doors have two enormous bronze knockers of great artistic value. However, to see the originals you'll need to visit the second chamber of the Giralda, where they are in safe keeping (see p. 138).

NEARBY

House of the Kreybigs

If you look up towards the beams of the colonnade at No. 9 Calle Alemanes you can see the inscription *Soi de Kreybig* (I belong to Kreybig). This is a reminder that in the 18th century Antonio Creivig lived here and ran his Bohemian glassware business.

Calle Alemanes is named after the tradesmen of Germanic origin who had their shops here, opposite the cathedral steps.

CROSS OF THE OATH

⑧

The place where traders sealed their deals

Calle Fray Ceferino González (no number)

On the north-facing side of the Archivo de Indias (Archive of the Indies, the former Casa Lonja de los Mercaderes, or Merchants' Market House), and opposite the cathedral's Puerta del Príncipe (Prince's

Entrance), stands a great cross made from jasper and marble. Erected in 1612, it's known as *Crux del juramento* (oath), because this was where traders and merchants would seal their deals, often relating to the sale of products brought on the ships arriving from the West Indies. A verbal oath sworn in public at the foot of the cross would stand as a pledge to meet the terms that had been agreed.

This wasn't its original location; as may be observed from old engravings, until the Lisbon earthquake of 1755 it stood outside the main façade of the market, in the middle of the so-called Plaza de la Lonja.

NEARBY
Casa Lonja de los Mercaderes ⑨
Archivo General de Indias – Avenida de la Constitución
Admission free, Tuesday–Saturday 9.30am–5pm, Sunday 10am–2pm

Before the merchants' market was built, traders made their deals in the area around the cathedral: on the steps outside or in the Patio de los Naranjos (Patio of the Orange Trees), and even inside the temple on wet or swelteringly hot days, eliciting the outrage of the cathedral chapter. In 1598 the continual complaints led Philip II to instigate the construction of a suitable location to host these commercial and financial transactions, and act as headquarters for the Consulado de Cargadores a Indias (Consulate of Traders with the Indies), the group of businessmen specialising in trade with the Americas, a monopoly that Seville held.

Following trade with the Indies' move to Cádiz, the Renaissance building underwent a period of neglect, and was even converted into tenement housing. During the reign of Charles III it was decided to renovate the building so it could house all the documents relating to the American colonies, thereby founding the Archivo General de Indias (General Archive of the Indies). The first carriages laden down with parchments arrived from Cádiz, Madrid and Simancas (Valladolid) in October 1785. The archive, whose shelves of Cuban mahogany are currently stacked with some 43,000 parchments, maps and drawings (the most valuable of which are stored in secure facilities), is a pilgrim site for scholars of the Americas and researchers from around the world, providing cover for the occasional shipwreck treasure-hunter.

Mystery of the mausoleum of the conquistador who died in Seville

Archivo General de Indias
Avenida de la Constitución
Tuesday–Saturday 9.30am–5pm & Sunday 10am–2pm
Admission free

At the top of the formidable 18th-century stairway in the former Casa Lonja de los Mercadores (Merchants' Market House), the current Archivo General de Indias (General Archive of the Indies), the landing to the left boasts the gilt effigy of the conquistador of Mexico, Hernán Cortés (1485–1547), depicting him in the style of a Roman emperor, dressed in a cuirass featuring medallions and acanthus leaves and wrapped in a cloak.

This bust, a copy of the original the Dukes of Monteleone (the conquistador's descendants and heirs) had in Sicily, was commissioned by Antoine d'Orléans, the Duke of Montpensier, who was obsessed by everything to do with Cortés. To such a degree that he renovated the rambling house in Castilleja de la Cuesta (Seville) where Hernán Cortés died aged 62, terminally ill and abandoned by the Spanish Crown, turning it into a summer house.

Cast in gilt bronze, the original bust came from the hand of Valencian artist Manuel Tolsá, who executed it in Mexico in 1792 for Cortés' mausoleum in the church of the Hospital de Jesús, a building founded by the conquistador at the location where he was supposed to have first met the Aztec emperor Moctezuma.

In 1823, two years after the Independence of Mexico, the mausoleum was dismantled to avoid it being desecrated. The remains of the conquistador were hidden in a niche in the wall of the church and, to deceive the agitators, the bust and coat of arms were sent to Italy. In 1922, the statue travelled from Palermo to Naples and is currently on display in the ballroom of the Villa Pignatelli museum, the palace of Hernán Cortés' heirs, the Aragona Pignatelli Cortés family.

Meanwhile, the remains of the Spanish conquistador were consigned to complete oblivion for over a hundred years. It wasn't until 1946 that an official discovered a document in a secret compartment in the vault of the Spanish embassy in Mexico City, clearing up one of the great mysteries of Mexican historiography. It turned out that the remains of the explorer and conquistador had been hidden behind a stone plaque on the wall of the high altar of the church of the Hospital de Jesús in Mexico, as requested in his last will and testament.

The Madre de Dios convent on Calle San José, founded by Queen Isabella I in the 15th century, houses the tombs and recumbent statues of Hernán Cortés' second wife, Juana de Zúñiga, and his daughters Catalina and Juana.

ALMOHAD PATIO IN CASA DE LA CONTRATACIÓN

A magnificent hidden medieval patio

Plaza de la Contratación, 3
secretaria.general.sevilla.dgob@juntadeandalucia.es
Visits by prior appointment, Wednesday afternoons

A building housing regional government offices acts as a hiding place for a magnificent medieval patio representing the beauty of Almohad architecture. This fantastic spot may be visited, by prior appointment, on Wednesday afternoons.

Cross the vestibule to enter a garden with paths forming the shape of a cross, enclosing four central reservoirs, which according to Islamic tradition drew inspiration from the rivers of paradise.

In the middle there would have been a fountain, filling the reservoirs and emanating freshness and the melodious sound of trickling water throughout the whole garden. The original beds were sunken almost 2 metres down, making it easy to pick oranges and other fruits, and heightening the enjoyment of the flora. These four sections are bordered by brick walls with blind arches that still feature the original paintings simulating wooden doors inside them.

The most iconic image of this space is the magnificent arcade of multifoil arches and sections of wall featuring decorative elements of interlinking geometric forms, a pattern known as *sebka*.

The patio constituted a central feature in one of the palatial residences that made up the Real Alcázar in the medieval Al-Andalus period. Although these gardens were reused and transformed shortly after the Christian conquest by the Castilian kings who lived in the Alcázar, in particular by Alfonso X and Peter I, they preserve a number of remarkable elements from Hispano-Islamic culture.

It was discovered in the 1960s, following the demolition of the old Casa de Contratación (House of Trade), which the Catholic Monarchs had built in 1503 to house the institution that monopolised commercial and travel links with the Americas. It remained here until its move to Cádiz in the 18th century, with the location going on to serve a range of functions, mainly related to the Real Alcázar.

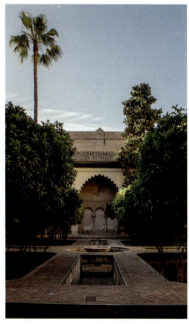

MOUNT PARNASSUS
IN THE JARDÍN DEL LABERINTO

Centre of the Old Maze of the Real Alcázar

Real Alcázar
Plaza del Triunfo
alcazarsevilla.org
Daily 9.30am–5pm (winter) & 9.30am–7pm (summer)
Admission free: Monday 6pm–7pm April–September & 4pm–5pm,
October–March

In the Maze Garden, also known as that of the *Cruz* (Cross), there is a pond with a mound made up of rocks, known as Mount Parnassus. This, unknown to most visitors (and even some of the guides here), was the centre of the Old Maze of the Real Alcázar.

To reach the site of the maze King Philip IV ordered to be built in 1627, you have to cross the garden of the *Damas* (Ladies) until you get to the door at the end of the wall, whose lintel features an allegorical painting of Theseus killing the Minotaur.

Water flows from the Hippocrene spring (see below) at the top of the mound, conceived of as a replica of Mount Parnassus in Greece. In a grotto lower down there are two female figures joined at their backs, from whose breasts water also flows.

The choice of these elements was by no means random, and acted to heighten the maze's symbolism, given that in Greek mythology both the mount and the spring were consecrated to the muses.

As with the oldest mazes, the idea was to reach the centre and then find your way out again. On arriving at Mount Parnassus, having wandered lost between the myrtle hedgerows, visitors would reach the font of Knowledge and Art, attributes they would take with them on finding their way out.

The hedges were trimmed using the art of topiary, forming fantastical figures and animals to which heads and hands of baked clay were added with the intention of unsettling visitors and generating terror in those who dared to enter.

The old maze stood on the same spot for 300 years, undergoing major modifications along the way. Its final destruction came in the 20th century on the express orders of Doña Maria Christina of Austria, the mother of Alfonso XIII, who didn't like seeing the ladies and gentlemen of the Court losing themselves.

Mount Parnassus

According to Greek legend the famous mount got its name from Parnassós, the son of Poseidon, and is considered the symbolic homeland of poets. Apollo lived there, to whom the Temple of Delphi is dedicated, the most spectacular shrine in the Ancient world, also located on this mountain in central Greece. Furthermore, legend tells us that Hippocrene (Spring of the Horse) was created in Mount Parnassus by blows received from Pegasus, the winged horse sent by Poseidon.

MAZE IN THE CENADOR DE LA ALCOBA

Mystery of the Renaissance tile

Pabellón de Carlos V
Real Alcázar
Plaza del Triunfo
alcazarsevilla.org
Daily 9.30am–5pm (winter) & 9.30am–7pm (summer)
Admission free: Monday 6pm–7pm, April–September & 4pm–5pm
October–March

On the floor of Charles V's spectacular pavilion, also known as the Cenador de la Alcoba (Arbour of the Bed Chamber), there is a tile featuring a mysterious maze.

Executed using the picado technique of inscribing with a sharp-ended tool, the maze is located at the foot of one of the windows, inserted into the room's magnificent Renaissance flooring. Of course, this design has nothing to do with the later 17th-century maze, with its winding passages and Parnassus pond at the centre, as may be seen from surviving plans of the Alcázar, such as the one by Van der Borcht (1759), or the plan of the city commissioned by Olavide (1771) (see p. 100). As for the tile on the pavilion floor, this is a classical square design of straight lines with a pattern of alternative routes and a space in the middle as the destination.

The origin of the pavilion, erected among orange trees by the Morisco Juan Fernández in 1546 as a place of repose for the emperor, may be a remodelling of an Islamic shrine (*qubba*), which might explain the origin of the name Huerta de la Alcoba (Garden of the Bed Chamber).

New maze of 1914

The new maze, the one open to the public, was built opposite the Cenador de la Alcoba in 1914 following the design found in the flooring of the pavilion, but adapting its square format to a rectangular one, with narrow passages between myrtle and cypress hedgerows.

SEVILLA. Jardines del Alcázar. El Labirinto

See double-page spread overleaf for more on mazes.

Origin and initiation symbolism of the maze

According to legend, Daedalus built one of the earliest mazes to imprison the Minotaur, a monster born of the love between Queen Pasiphaë, the wife of King Minos of Greece, and a bull. Some archaeologists hold that the complex floorplan of Minos' palace in Knossos (Greece) may have been the origin of the legend. Only three people managed to get out. The first was Theseus, who went to Crete to kill the monster. Having fallen in love with Theseus, Minos' daughter Ariadne gave him a ball of thread so he could find his way back (Ariadne's famous string). The other two were Daedalus and his son, Icarus, after Minos imprisoned Daedalus in his own labyrinth. According to some versions the king did this in order to avoid the plan of the maze being revealed, while others argue it was punishment for having given Ariadne the idea of the ball of thread. The design was so perfect that the only solution Daedalus came up with was to escape through the air, with the help of wings he fashioned for himself and Icarus out of wax and feathers. Although many civilisations have drawn or engraved labyrinths (Mesopotamia, Egypt, the Hopi and Navajo Native Americans), they have been present in Europe since prehistoric times. Reintroduced by Christianity, mazes enabled those

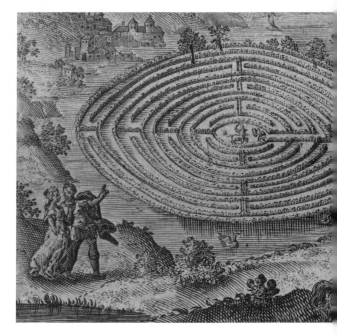

who could not physically undertake the pilgrimage to Jerusalem to do so symbolically, working their way through to the centre on their knees. Normally located on the western side of the nave, the direction from which devils came (west is the direction of death, where the Sun sets), these church mazes made it possible to capture them before they reached the choir, as they could supposedly only move in a straight line. Symbolically, the maze expressed mankind's progression within himself. After a necessary journey of initiation, often painful and tortuous, he finds his lost sense of unity, something that had split between a multitude of desires and paths. Arrival at the centre of the maze marks the end of the initiation. The flight of Daedalus and Icarus symbolises the elevation of the spirit towards knowledge, and that of the soul towards God (and success in the fight against the Minotaur, which symbolises our nature and our animal impulses), and Ariadne's love for Theseus symbolises love for another being. Two ways of escaping the absurdity of the human condition. If the wax in Icarus' wings ends up melting because he flies too close to the Sun, that is because his pride, dictated by an overly intellectual stance, makes him believe he is on a par with the gods.

WATER ORGAN AT FUENTE DE LA FAMA

One of three organ fountains in Europe

Real Alcázar
Puerta del León
Calle Miguel Mañara
alcazarsevilla.org
Daily 9.30am–5pm October–March & 9.30am–7pm April–September
Admission free Monday 4pm–5pm October–March & 6pm–7pm
April–September
Organ music: every hour on the hour

On entering the Alcázar gardens by the stairs that lead on from the Fountain of Mercury, alongside the Gallery of the Grotesque you'll find the Fountain of Fame, the only surviving 17th-century organ fountain in Spain. This is one of just three in Europe, the other two being in Italy, at the Villa d'Este in Tivoli and the Quirinal palace in Rome.

The Fountain of Fame owes its name to the figure that presides over it, which carried a trumpet that has since disappeared. It was conceived of as a structure capable of housing a water organ in what has been known, since Greek times, as a *camera aeolia* (wind chamber), at the back. To spot the organ you have to look through the orifices in the chamber door, just to the right of the fountain. In this area, if you look up you'll also see a grille over the Gallery of the Grotesque. The purpose of these openings is none other than to enable the music emitted by the 70 organ pipes to reach every corner of the garden.

The fountain is remarkable in its size and monumental stature, giving the impression of being part of the gallery with which it shares it grotesque style of decoration. The arrangement of various rows of benches in front of it elevates the fountain to the level of theatre stage. The papyrus plants that populate it, concealing the water spouts, act as the curtain.

When the clock strikes the hour the area around the fountain is transformed into a little concert hall. The water spouts seem to turn into dancers who move to the rhythm of the music. The water organ is punctual in starting up, and the notes it emits may be heard for a few minutes throughout most of the garden. It plays two short pieces by the 17th-century composer Francisco Correa de Arauxo: Opus LXVIII *Canto Llano de la Inmaculada Concepción de la Virgen María* (Plainchant of the Immaculate Conception of the Virgin Mary), and *Siguense Dies y Seis Glosas sobre el Canto Llano* (Here follow Sixteen Glosas based on the Plainchant).

The combination of air and water to produce musical sounds was first conceived of by the Greek inventor from the 2nd century BCE, Ctesibius. In the Renaissance the mechanism was rediscovered, reaching the Alcázar thanks to its conservator Vermondo Resta. Over the years this curious instrument, also known as a *Hydraulis*, was abandoned until 2006 when it was restored by English expert Rodney Briscoe, the conservator of all three surviving organs in Europe, bringing music back to the gardens.

BATHS OF MARÍA DE PADILLA

The favourite spot of the woman who became queen after her death

Real Alcázar
Puerta del León
Calle Miguel Mañara
alcazarsevilla.org
Daily 9.30am–5pm October–March & 9.30am–7pm April–September
Admission free Monday 4pm–5pm October–March & 6pm–7pm
April–September

A tunnel from the Jardín de la Danza (Dance Garden) winds its way under the foundations of the Gothic palace, leading to a secluded and magical spot that seems frozen in time. The orange-tinged light filtering from the ceiling blurs into the silent body of water covered by three stone galleries, making up the baths of María de Padilla.

This is an Almohad *aljibe* (underground water reservoir), which formed part of a sunken garden designed 5 metres below the rest of the palace for use in the hot summer months. In the 13th century Alfonso X, known as 'the Wise', ordered it be covered by a Gothic rib vault.

According to legend, this was the favourite place of María de Padilla, the lover of King Peter I (see p. 104). The fact is, in the summer the temperature here is several degrees lower than in the rest of the city. María moved in with the king, taking up residence in the Real Alcázar in 1352 and bearing four of his children. Although Peter I officially married two other women for political reasons, when María de Padilla died in 1361 he forced the Archbishop of Toledo to annul those marriages and consecrate the secret wedding he had had with his lover, with witnesses present.

We can be sure about that secret wedding from 1352, as there is a Royal Privilege by which María de Padilla was granted the city of Huelva as a wedding gift. As such, Parliament recognised her as queen, ensuring that the children she bore would be legitimate, and that she could be buried in the Royal Chapel of Seville Cathedral, where she lies to this day. That at one time this space was put to recreational use became quite apparent following the 1997 discovery, and subsequent restoration, of some Renaissance mural paintings that had been hidden by damp and decay. The delicate polychrome works, which are not currently available to visit, were executed between 1565 and 1579, and depict agricultural and hunting scenes, along with other subjects from courtly life.

María de Padilla, queen of magic

The figure of María de Padilla has had quite an impact on collective cultural imagination over the centuries, from the popular romances that were widespread throughout the Iberian Peninsula to the opera bearing her name premiered by Donizetti in Milan's Scala in 1841. Perhaps oddest of all is her assimilation as queen of magic in Brazilian religions of African origin, where she is considered a powerful and terrible seductive she-devil.

Legend of the beautiful Jewish girl who betrayed her own people

Calle Susona, 10 A

Down a narrow alley in the Santa Cruz district, a tile featuring a bare skull is a reminder of the legend of a beautiful Jewish girl who betrayed her own people.

Known as Calle Susona since 1845, this street was previously called Calle de la Muerte (Death Street), which is how it appears on Olavide's 1771 city plan (see p. 100), and as can also be seen from the Baroque tile at the start of the road.

In 1248, the year Seville was conquered by the Christians, when

Ferdinand III entered the city he found it empty; all the inhabitants had fled. Later all the mosques would be handed over the Church, except for three that Ferdinand's son, Alfonso X, granted to the Jewish community to establish their synagogues. In the late 14th century, following the attacks on the Jewish quarter, said synagogues became the churches of San Bartolomé, Santa María la Blanca and Santa Cruz, with the latter giving its name to the district.

Years later, some of the Jewish families returned, joining large numbers of newly converted Christian *conversos* who had turned their back on Judaism, though some of them continued to practise their faith in secret. One such was the banker Diego de Susón, a member of a large group of prominent citizens extremely concerned by the huge pressure they were under since the Inquisition began in 1478. His house in the old Jewish quarter was one of the places where bankers, businessmen and civil servants would meet, even going so far as to discuss a possible armed uprising. His daughter, Susana Ben Susón (nicknamed La Susona), who also lived in the house, became an unwilling witness to the conspiracy, leading her to betray her father to a Christian knight with whom she had relations, leading to the arrest of all those involved.

On 6 February 1481 Seville witnessed its first execution by burning, with six convicted prisoners from the group of Jewish *conversos* burned at the stake in Tablada. This was followed by a slew of arrests and further summary executions. According to tradition, remorse at having betrayed her family and her people led La Susona to enter a convent, with her last will and testament reading as follows: '*when I have died, my head should be severed from my body and nailed over the door of my house where it should stay forever*'. And so it was, until the beginning of the 17th century, which is why it was called Death Street. After the house was renovated in 1931, a little tile was put up to replace the iron hook that was supposed to have held her head.

STONE PLAQUE
OF WASHINGTON IRVING

Reminder of the Romantic traveller in the former Residencia de América

Calle del Agua, 2

The North American writer and diplomat Washington Irving (New York, 1783 – Tarrytown, NY, 1859) was one of the precursors of the Romantic discovery of southern Spain in the mid-19th century.

In tribute to the writer, a commemorative relief plaque was put up on the wall of a beautiful palace looking over the Callejón del Agua alley, next to the wall of the Real Alcázar, and which barely merits a second glance from passers-by in the Santa Cruz district. Few are aware that in 1925 this building was the Residencia de América, thus linked with the American writer, whose time in Granada is much better known though it was really in Seville that his Andalusian travels began.

The bronze plaque, executed in 1925 by the brilliant sculptor Mariano Benlliure, depicts the writer half-length and looking straight ahead, turned to the right, with short hair and ample sideburns and dressed in a jacket and cravat. The relief was commissioned by the Marquis de la Vega-Inclán, who was in charge of revamping the Santa Cruz district for the 1929 Expo.

A hundred years earlier, the writer was living in Seville, right there in Santa Cruz, the old Jewish quarter, while writing his *Tales of the Alhambra*. In spring 1828 he arrived at the city's port on board the *Betis*, the first Spanish steamship, which went up the Guadalquivir from Cádiz. He stayed in the city for a year, an experience recorded in his diary published by the Hispanic Society of New York: *Diary of Washington Irving of the Sunnyside Spain*. His daily life in the city included his immersion in the works, cartography and other documents in the Archive of the Indies and the Library of Ferdinand Columbus, an endeavour that would culminate in *A History of the Life and Voyages of Christopher Columbus*.

But like any Romantic traveller worth his salt, the writer fell in love with the Andalusian heritage, with all the tradition predating the Christian conquest of the city, added to the discovery that it was only a few days' journey to the city of Granada, with its magnificent palace of the Alhambra, the red fortress.

Route of Washington Irving

legadoandalusi.es/las-rutas/ruta-de-washington-irving

This route follows in the footsteps of the Romantic writer's 1829 journey, taking in the cities of Seville and Granada, fascinated by the richness and exoticism of the Hispano-Islamic legacy.

DEVIL'S GRILLE

An impossible cast-iron work

Palacio de Pickman
Plaza de Alfaro, 1

On the front of the palatial residence of the Marquises de Pickman, there is an intricate and curiously designed piece of iron latticework on the left-hand corner window. The bars of the *reja del diablo* (devil's grille), interlink with each other, tongue and grooving from one square to the next without there being any visible soldering or any other method of binding them together. The way this grille was assembled makes it one of the most complicated surviving models of this

particular technique, due to the way that the grooved ends are arranged, most of all because said apertures were made in the corner edges of the bars, rather than in the flat cross-pieces, as was more common. An impossible feat of ironwork that led some to comment it must have been cast in the fires of hell.

Door transported one stone at a time

Apart from the grille, the most interesting feature of the Palacio de Pickman is its imposing 16th-century Renaissance entrance, executed in plateresque style, visible behind a high railing in the main façade of neighbouring Calle Lope de Rueda. This doorway comes from the palace of the Aranda family in Úbeda (Jaén), from where it was transported in the 1920s, one stone at a time. It features two stone sections with profuse decoration including rampant lions, rams, masks, infants and so on.

Journey from civil graveyard to Catholic cemetery and back again ...

The Pickman family, owners of the house that bears their name, are descendants of the English impresario Charles Pickman, who in 1838 chose La Cartuja monastery as the site for his famous ceramics factory (see p. 276). In recognition of his endeavours, King Amadeo I granted him the rank of marquis. Some years later, María de las Cuevas Pickman, the impresario's only granddaughter and sole heiress to the family title and fortune, married Rafael de León y Primo de Rivera. Her husband, from a noble Córdoba family fallen on hard times, was a great lover of the high life and worldly pleasures, and following a disagreement with a commander from the Civil Guard over debts in the Teatro Cervantes, the marquis was killed in a duel on 10 October 1904. Considered a suicide by the Church, Archbishop Spínola would not allow his body to be buried on consecrated ground, thereby forcing him to be interred in the civil cemetery. On the day of his burial, an entourage of hundreds of workers broke into the Catholic cemetery intent on laying his body to rest in the family pantheon, only for it to be returned to the civil graveyard once more by government decree.

NEARBY
Balcone di Rosina

Rossini premiered his *opera buffa* (comic opera) *The Barber of Seville* in Rome in 1816. The main character Rosina's encounters with her lover, conducted from a Seville balcony, were the inspiration for the owner of this house to build this beautiful feature in 1928. Another addition was the entranceway from a 17th-century palace in Écija (Seville).

ORIGINAL DOORWAY TO THE ALCÁZAR

The secret entrance

Foro de la Biodiversidad
Patio de Banderas, 16
954 21 14 17
Tuesday–Sunday 10am–9pm
Admission free

I n 1999, when the 19th-century building at No. 16 Patio de Banderas was renovated for use as office space, the archaeologists undertaking the works made a surprising discovery. Hidden behind a wall was an impressive door with ironwork, subsequently identified as the original entrance to the Alcázar.

On view in the building's conference hall, the doorway stands 9 metres tall, and is flanked on both sides by turrets made from stone blocks. The vault of the archway features two ceramic *buzones matafuegos*, apertures akin to murder holes or machicolations, used to pour water from the walls and put out any attempt at fire during a siege.

Curiously, when three of the stone slabs were removed from the floor during the renovation works, a Latin inscription was found on the underside from part of a 2nd-century commemorative pedestal dedicated to the goddess Minerva by the guild of oil-traders of Hispalis (Roman Seville). It was then converted for use as an altar table or funerary headstone in the Palaeochristian and Visigothic period from the 5th to 7th centuries.

Calle Joaquín Romero Murube runs along the other side of this blind doorway, where an archway can be detected in the wall, below street level and often covered by vegetation. This was the original entrance to the 11th-century Islamic Alcázar, which also provided access to the city. It was later blocked off following the Almoravid expansion works and the Almohad urban reforms to the port area in the 12th century, with the entrance to the city relocated to the Puerta de Jerez.

Until Calle Joaquín Romero Murube was opened in the 1960s, access to the Santa Cruz district, the old Jewish quarter, was via the side entrance to the Patio de Banderas, which had for many years been used as tenement housing.

Seville at its oldest

The age of this area has been certified by archaeological digs carried out in the Patio de Banderas, which have made it possible to discover the oldest remains of human activity found in Seville to date. Such findings include the bottom of an oven or stove dating to the 8th century BCE, at the end of the Bronze Age. Historians consider this to be the origin of the Andalusian capital, at that time still on the seashore. Another curious discovery was a relief of a phallus with the tail of a lion and two bovine legs in movement, possibly indicating that a Roman building was being used as a brothel.

PLAZA DE SANTA MARTA

A secret and magical oasis

Plaza de Santa Marta

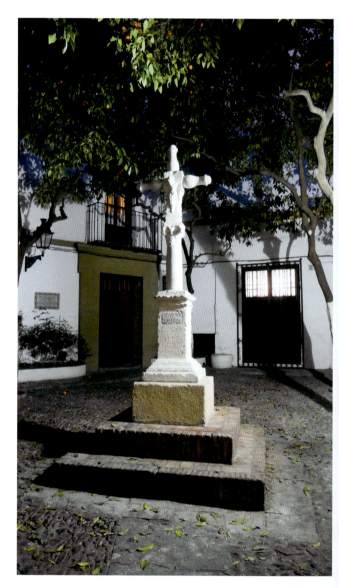

On going down a dead-end alleyway, or *adarve* as they were known in Medieval Spain, you stumble upon a magical spot called Plaza de Santa Marta, a little trapezoidal square which in spring engulfs visitors with the scent of jasmine and orange blossom.

This tiny square is a real oasis, hidden amidst the bustle of the cathedral quarter. In the centre is a stone Cross, around which six orange trees stand guard (the tallest ones in Seville, because the narrow nature of the square means they have to grow upwards in search of light). The Renaissance Calvary Cross, which features a crucified Christ on one side and a Pietà on the other, was designed by Hernán Ruiz (responsible for the Giralda bell tower) and sculpted by Diego de Alcaraz in the 16th century.

The Cross has been given the name San Lázaro, because in 1564 it was erected on the outskirts of the city, opposite the leper colony of San Lázaro (see p. 288), on the royal highway from the monastery of San Jerónimo.

On the way out, the left-hand wall of the alleyway still features remains of the old Los Osos mosque: two windows with multi-foil arches and a pointed internal blind arch. This mosque must have been a major building, given how near it was to the Real Alcázar, and may have served as a local shrine prior to the 1198 construction of the nearby great mosque with its minaret (the present-day Giralda). When the city was conquered by the Christians in 1248, the mosque was taken over by the cathedral chapter, which in 1385 granted it to Ferrán Martínez, Archdean of Écija and instigator of the uprisings that signalled the demise of Seville's Jewish quarter six years later (see p. 184). Here he founded the Mudéjar-style hospital of Santa Marta, which centuries later would take in the Augustinian nuns who were thrown out of the convent of the Encarnación in 1811 following the French occupation, when it was demolished to make way for the market bearing its name. The name of the convent moved along with the nuns.

Legend has it that Don Juan Tenorio kidnapped Doña Inés within the walls of this square.

Pieces of the Blessed Sacrament

In the convent of La Encarnación, at No. 3 Plaza del Triunfo, you can acquire thin, white wafers of unleavened bread, clearly unconsecrated, made every day by the nuns using artisan techniques. A timeless tradition that still lives on in the city.

CASA DE LAS CONCHAS

Almost a hundred different rosettes

Calle Mateos Gago, 26

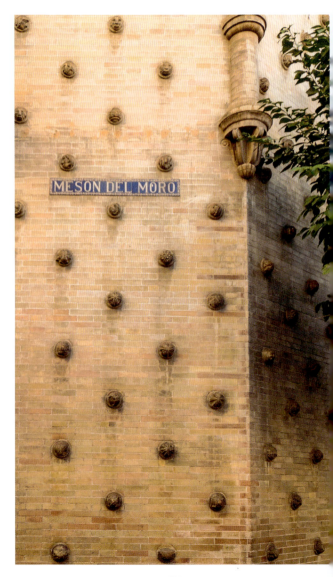

At the intersection between the two streets Mesón del Moro and Mateos Gago there is a strange Regionalist-style building dating from 1917. The work of local architect Aníbal González, its façade is dotted with almost a hundred little rosettes made from carved brick, each one with a different design.

Of the huge number of reliefs on view, there is actually only one shell, lost among animals (birds, a horse, an owl ...), human figures (musicians, native Indians ...), plant motifs, allegorical ones ...

The name it has been popularly given in Seville, is due to its similarities with the famous House of Shells in Salamanca.

NEARBY

Mesón del Moro's Arab bathhouse

Mesón del Moro, 6

Located on the site where the main gateway to the Jewish quarter used to be, a building currently converted into a restaurant houses the best-preserved Arab baths in Seville. Dating back to the 12th century, they would have served some nearby mosque, such as the Los Osos one (see p. 172). The baths subsequently became part of the historic 'Meson del Moro' (Moor's Inn), which gave its name to the street and was created in 1495 with a privilege issued by the Catholic Monarchs allowing it to accommodate Muslim travellers visiting the city.

Bar Giralda's hammam

Mateos Gago, 1

Recent building works have uncovered an Almohad hammam with a series of mural paintings of great quality, and unique in Spain. This Islamic bathhouse still preserves its cool room and its warm room, the most luxurious and impressive one, the remains of an arch marking the warm water room, and the door of the main entrance, which was where Calle Don Remondo is today. Also worth highlighting are the 88 miniature skylights of different sizes and shapes. Dating from the first quarter of the 12th century, these baths were the closest to what was then the *aljama* (Almohad mosque), where the city's cathedral now stands.

ESCUELA DE CRISTO

Secret square in the Santa Cruz district

Calle Don Carlos Alonso Chaparro
Sunday & public holidays 11am

In the maze that is the Santa Cruz district, there is a tiny little square unknown to both locals and outsiders, which is home to one of the oddest and most secretive institutions created in the Baroque period: the School of Christ. Head down an alleyway just off Calle Ximénez de Enciso and pass under the gateway at the end, and you'll find yourself in a secluded little square with the school chapel on the left. The whitewashed walls with their flower pots, the cast-iron cross on its white marble pillar,

the orange and lemon trees, ceramic altarpieces ... all these elements lend it a particular flavour.

Established in 1793, the Escuela de Cristo de la Natividad (School of Christ of the Nativity) is the only one that has survived of the three that once existed in Seville, and currently has around 20 brothers. The institution was founded in Madrid in the mid-17th century by the Sicilian Oratorian Juan Bautista Ferruzzo, for the purposes of promoting a more austere and introspective spirituality. Each of what were once more than 400 schools is presided over by a priest known as the Padre Obediencia (Father Obedience). Members were limited to a maximum of 72, at most 24 ordained and 48 lay brothers, this being the same number as Christ's disciples (see below). Exceeding this number meant the founding of a new school. As in all Escuelas de Cristo, this chapel is presided over by a *Stabat Mater* consisting of a Crucified Christ and a Virgin Mary kneeling at his feet, which is where the brothers would undertake their exercises, meditations and mortifications of the flesh by candlelight. Until the 1960s, when these acts of discipline were still being carried out, two skulls would be placed at the foot of the altar along with a cross made up of two tibias. These human bones are now kept in a casket in the chapel. Notable among the artworks preserved here is a little Crucified Christ, a piece dating to the late 15th century and attributed to the painter of religious images Pedro Millán, which features the unusual detail that the blood is represented by red glass. The school also boasts two nativity scenes of great value. One of the brothers discovered a curious secret in the 18th-century nativity by Cristóbal Ramos: the names of the brothers at the school who had died were written on little tablets concealed in the most symbolic place – under the cushions in the Infant Christ's manger.

Christ's 72 disciples

The 72 disciples, known in the Eastern Christian tradition as the Seventy Apostles, were the first emissaries of Jesus, as mentioned in the Gospel of Luke (10: 1–24).

A door at the front of the square leads into the sacristy of the church of Santa Cruz, which then opens out onto Calle Mateos Gago.

LAST SECTION OF THE JEWISH QUARTER'S WALL

Protected by millstones

Calle Fabiola, 1

The Jewish quarter (*judería*) constituted a city within a city, separated by a wall that protected it from threats and possible attacks. On Calle Fabiola the last vestiges of the inner wall that ran from the Alcázar and linked up with the city's outer wall can be seen. At the foot of this section is a row of millstones, used to protect the wall from damage caused by the axle shafts of passing carriages. Just how widespread this sort of protective

barrier was in the old town bears witness to the sheer quantity of mills that operated along the rivers of Seville.

The wall enclosed the current parish churches of Santa Cruz, San Bartolomé and Santa María la Blanca. These correspond to the three mosques which, in 1252 after the Christian conquest, Alfonso X granted to his Jewish advisers and treasurers so they could serve as the synagogues of their community, who were mostly from Toledo.

The entrances in the wall were closed at nightfall, protecting the nigh-on 500 families who lived there, some 3,000 people accounting for a tenth of the population of Seville. Opposite the church of San Nicolás was one of the internal doorways connecting with the rest of the city, and opening out onto the Jewish quarter's main thoroughfare, where Calle San José is today, ending at the Puerta de la Carne gateway. This gateway, formerly known as Perlas (Pearls) or Minjoar (under Islamic rule), was the main exit in the outside wall, providing access to the countryside and Jewish cemetery. Another gateway, in what is now Calle Judería, was the road to the royal enclosure in the Alcázar. In their *aljama* (self-governing quarter), the Jews had their own jurisdiction and authorities, though they paid special taxes to both the Crown and Church. The professional community was dominated by doctors, apothecaries, merchants, artisans, money-lenders, money-changers and so on.

The late 14th century saw a series of violent attacks instigated by the preacher Ferrán Martínez, causing the death and flight of many of the inhabitants of the *judería*. From that point on, the district began to disappear as an enclosed space, and over the years its walls and gateways were pulled down (the Puerta de la Carne in the 19th century), with new spaces and streets opening up.

Its urban layout still survives today, with a few remains (see map) recalling the legacy of the Jews that lived in Seville, who at that time had to exile themselves from their homeland, Sefarad.

For more vestiges of the *judería*, see double-page spread overleaf.

Vestiges of the *judería*

Apart from the section of wall described earlier and its key (see opposite), there are few surviving vestiges of Seville's Jewish *aljama*. It did have three major synagogues, each established in a former mosque following the Christian conquest of the city in the 13th century. They would be reconverted into Christian churches a century later. Santa María la Blanca (Calle Santa María la Blanca, 5) was the most important synagogue in Seville, converting into a Christian church after the attacks on the *judería* in 1391. This is the only temple to have preserved remains from the three religions: some of its walls have been identified as belonging to the old

mosque. The arches in the central nave, covered with plaster in the Baroque period, are those of the Mudéjar synagogue, whose floorplan largely matched that of the present-day church. At the side entrance on Calle Archeros (so-called because this was where the royal guard, known as *archeros*, was accommodated at the marriage of Charles V), two Roman pillars still stand, crowned by Visigothic capitals that would have originally supported the arches of the synagogue. The second synagogue became the church of Santa Cruz in the 13th century and, following its demolition in the 19th century, it was transformed into the current Plaza de Santa Cruz. Four pillars from the synagogue have survived, preserved in the great railings surrounding the gardens of the Pabellón de Chile (see p. 242). The last Jewish temple was pulled down at the end of the 18th century to make way for the church of San Bartolomé (see p. 185). This was located in the neighbourhood that has perhaps preserved the most genuinely Sephardic feel in its maze-like streets and narrow alleys. To see it, just walk down Calle Verde or Calle Levíes, which takes its name from an important Jewish family that had a palatial residence here.

Key to the judería

Kept in the Cathedral Treasury, the key to the *judería* is made from gilt silver, and its bit bears the inscription *Dios abrirá, Rey entará*, meaning 'God will open, the King will enter'. It features a die-shaped cube between the eyelet and the shaft, with a ship, a galley, a spherical knot and castles and lions engraved on its faces. It also has another inscription, this time in Arabic: 'The King of Kings will open, the King of the Earth will enter' on the side edging. In an attempt to gain royal protection, this key was handed over to Ferdinand III by prominent members of the *judería* when he made his symbolic entrance into the city one month after Seville had surrendered, on 23 November 1248. The Muslim commander Axataf had previously knelt before the monarch, also presenting him with the key to the city as a sign of fealty. That key is preserved alongside the Jewish one.

BOMB AT MAÑARA'S PALACE

When fire and shrapnel rained down for eight days

Dirección General de Bienes Culturales. Junta de Andalucía
Calle Levíes, 27
955 03 67 33 – visitas.altamira.ccul@juntadeandalucía.es
Guided tours Tuesday & Thursday 11am–12.30pm (includes entry to Palace of Altamira)
Admission free

On the left of the entrance to Miguel Mañara's Renaissance palace, just above an old tile belonging to an insurance company, visitors

are confronted with the odd spectacle of a little spherical bomb. This is a souvenir of the bombardment of the city by General Espartero's troops in the mid-19th century.

General Baldomero Espartero was a popular Spanish army officer who distinguished himself in the various wars of independence in the Americas and by winning the first Carlist war. He also proved an authoritarian regent of the realm in the years before Isabella II came of age, causing uprisings in many cities across the country, including Seville.

Faced with a possible attack, the citizens of the city joined forces with the Town Council and decided to arm themselves and fortify their defences. On 18 July 1843, the look-outs stationed on the top of the Giralda raised the alarm on spotting the regent's troops. For eight consecutive days, fire and shrapnel rained down on Seville from artillery positions located opposite two of the city wall gateways: Osario and Carmona. More than 600 shells and 900 round shot cannons were fired during the siege, mainly around the Carne and Osario gateways and the districts of San Bernardo and San Bartolomé, leaving many houses in ruins and streets full of rubble, not to mention the mass fatalities and injuries.

The residents of the city refused to come to any terms of surrender, determined either to 'triumph or perish', making do with few resources and limited military experience. A lack of political support meant that on 28 July Espartero ceased hostilities against Seville and went into exile in England. As a reward for its heroic defence, the government granted the city the title 'Invictus' in the name of Isabella II, and included a civic crown on its coat of arms.

Mañara's palace

In 1623 a Genovese merchant called Tomás Mañara bought and modernised this Renaissance palace, one of the most prominent buildings in the city. It was here that his son Miguel was born, the man behind the Brotherhood of Holy Charity. In the 18th and 19th centuries it was put to all sorts of uses: domestic, military (during the French invasion it was Marshal Soult's barracks), manufacturing, religious and, finally, educational. In 1989 it was purchased by the Junta de Andalucía as its administrative headquarters.

Origin of the name Calle Levíes

The name of the street is a reference to a Jewish family of noble lineage which had its palace here in the 14th century, and whose most famous member was Samuel Leví, treasurer to King Peter I.

JEWISH FOUNTAIN IN THE PALACE OF ALTAMIRA

One of the few vestiges of Seville's medieval judería

Consejería de Cultura, Junta de Andalucía
Santa María La Blanca, 1
955 03 67 33 – visitas.altamira.ccul@juntadeandalucía.es
Guided tours: non-public holiday Thursday 11am (includes entry to Mañara's palace)
Admission free

Considered one of the few vestiges of the city's medieval *judería* (Jewish quarter), a beautiful 14th-century fountain featuring

alicatado tiling may be found in a room on the left of the patio at the entrance to the Palace of Altamira.

This secret gem was uncovered thanks to building works relating to the palace's current use as office space. Some impressive polychrome Mudéjar coffered ceilings were also recovered.

One of the most important houses in the old Jewish quarter once stood on the site now occupied by the palace, located just down Dos Hermanas alleyway. This fountain may be the sole surviving element from the original Jewish home, a silent witness to some terrible events in the history of the city, now abandoned.

The house's first owner was Yusuf Pichón, a member of a wealthy family appointed Contador Mayor Real (Chief Royal Bookkeeper) by Henry II in 1371, an important position in the Hacienda Pública (Public Tax Office). Eight years later Pichón was murdered during celebrations to mark the coronation of King John I, in a plot involving both fellow Jews and Castilian nobles. At that time, Jews were granted the privilege to enforce blood justice among themselves, for which they needed an *albalá*, a royal authorisation signed by the king without knowing who the condemned man was. When the king found out that Don Yusuf had been beheaded, he ordered those behind the killing to be executed and revoked said privilege.

The house would later pass on to another Jewish Chief Bookkeeper, Samuel Abravanel, who became a *converso* and changed his name to Juan Sánchez de Sevilla during the terrible persecutions inflicted on those of his faith.

The great pogrom suffered by Seville's Jewish population in 1391, following years of anti-Jewish preaching by the Archdean of Écija, Ferrán Martínez, gave rise to the sacking of houses in the *judería* and the death of a large number of its inhabitants. As such, in 1397 the *converso* Juan Sánchez had no choice but to sell his houses to Diego López de Stúñiga, Justicia Mayor (Chief Magistrate) of the realm. The latter would subsequently build the mansion that would one day become the Palace of Altamira.

NEARBY

The last synagogue (26)
Calle Virgen de la Alegría, 2

The neo-classical church of San Bartolomé was built on the site of the last synagogue in Seville, demolished in 1779. It had previously been reused as a church after a Royal Decree ordered the devastated Jewish quarter be renovated and its three synagogues converted (see p. 180). Narrow streets such as Calle Verde or Calle Archeros are reminders of the medieval *judería*'s urban layout.

CERAMIC ALTARPIECE
OF SAINT FERDINAND III

One of the few surviving Baroque ceramic panels

Calle Cano y Cueto, 7

Hidden away towards the top of a 17th-century patio house at No.
7 Calle Cano y Cueto, there is an impressive mid-18th-century
ceramic altarpiece dedicated to Ferdinand III of Castile. This exceptional
piece, made in Triana by an unknown artist, is one of the few surviving

Baroque ceramic altarpieces, as the Town Council ordered the removal of almost all the public altars and holy images in the city in the 19th century.

The altarpiece features the king seen from the front, against a simple background of ochres and blues, his right hand holding his famous sword 'Lobera' (preserved in the Museo Catedralicio), and with an orb of the world in his left, alluding to his sovereign power.

His regal symbols are an ermine cloak and a gold crown with gemstones, with a cross on a globe at the top. He wears the Maltese Cross on top of his cuirass. His saintly condition is shown by his nimbus, a golden halo around his head.

Legend of the first time the saint-king slept in Seville

According to a popular tradition as curious as it's old, the king spent the night in a house here, next to where the Puerta de la Carne once stood, before his entrance into Seville on 22 December 1248, at the end of the one-month period of grace the Muslim population had been given to abandon the city.

This led to the nickname '*casa de una noche*' ('house of one night'). The altarpiece probably gave rise to the legend, rather than historical fact.

Procession of the Lobera sword

From the point at which the body of Ferdinand III was laid to rest in a tomb in the royal chapel of Seville cathedral, popular devotion to him would continue to grow until he was canonised in 1671, subsequently becoming the patron saint of the city. Ancestral rites commemorating the monarch still exist today, such as the procession of his sword, which was introduced by his son Alfonso X in 1255, whereby on 23 November the mayor of the city walks through each of the cathedral naves holding the sword by its tip.

Puerta de la Carne

Nothing remains of this gateway, located at the intersection of Calle Santa María la Blanca and Calle Cano y Cueto, which was demolished in 1864. It was the city wall's main gateway to the Jewish quarter, and its name originated in the mid-15th century, having been built near to the meat (*carne*) market that stood outside the wall.

SEPHARDIC TOMB

The medieval Jewish cemetery inside a car park

Parking Cano y Cueto
Calle Cano y Cueto, 2
Daily 24 hours

On the first floor of the car park next to the north entrance to the Murillo gardens, opposite parking space 9 and to the right of the ramp as you go in, there is a great big cylinder made from bricks on display behind a glass screen.

Uncovered along with a large number of buried bodies during building works from 1996 to 1997, this little-known archaeological treasure is nothing less than a medieval Jewish tomb. Once the discovered remains had been examined and were taken away, the decision was fortunately made to leave one tomb to bear witness to the find.

The tomb left on exhibit, which features a slightly trapezoidal coffin built out of bricks and shaped like a half-barrel vault, is perfectly preserved. The corpse was placed lying face up with its arms stretched out on both sides of the body, the palms of its hands face down, with its skull pointing west by north-west and its face towards the east and Jerusalem in accordance with Mosaic law.

This Jewish cemetery was installed outside the city wall near the gateway to the *judería*, also known as the Puerta de Minjoar and, subsequently, the Puerta de la Carne, until it was demolished in 1864 (see p. 179).

The origin of the Seville Jewish community's main necropolis can be traced back to the founding of the *aljama* in around 1250, after the Christian conquest of the city, and it continued to serve its purpose until the community's final departure from the city in the summer of 1484. There are, however, records of *conversos* being interred there at later dates in accordance with Jewish rites. The burial ground stretched from this area to the San Bernardo district. Its importance is borne out by the fact that this excavation uncovered almost 200 tombs, adding to the 146 that were found in 1992 during the building works on the nearby Diputación Provincial (Provincial Government).

In this same cemetery, but in an area where there were no Jewish tombs, archaeologists were surprised to come across a series of buried bodies of slaves from the modern era (16th and early 17th centuries) with clearly black ethnic features.

MIGUELETE

Weather vane on the Fábrica de Artillería

Avenida Eduardo Dato, 58

Many would probably fail to notice him, given how high up he is. Vigilantly scanning the skies of the San Bernardo district, a soldier uses his fixed bayonet to indicate the wind direction from the top of the main tower of the old Real Fábrica de Artillería (Royal Artillery Factory).

Made in the second half of the 18th century, this great iron and copper weather vane depicts a uniformed artilleryman, popularly known as Miguelete, carrying a sabre and a musket with bayonet. The end of the gun indicates the wind direction due to the force exerted on the spread of Miguelete's dress coat.

The two hundred years the weather vane spent subjected to every possible climatic excess finally took their toll, and it was restored in 2019.

The Real Fábrica de Artillería was a major complex of buildings intended for industrial and weapons-related use. After the complex fell into disrepair following closure in 1991, it underwent far-reaching renovation, converting into a cultural and artistic centre. Underneath the royal coat of arms, the elegant Baroque entrance is presided over by a clock that marks the facility's fabrication dates. This is dedicated to Baoiz and Velarde, the heroes of 2nd of May, who gave their names to the lions cast here to guard the entrance to the Congress of Deputies.

Juan Morel founded his Fundición de Campanas y Cañones (Bells and Cannons Foundry) here in 1565, and his successor, Bartolomé Morel, made the Giraldillo and a number of bells for the Giralda. In 1634 it became the property of the Spanish Crown, and at the end of the 18th century it underwent major renovation works leaving the magnificent Baroque building seen today.

This factory has been witness to key moments in world history. The cannons that defended the Caribbean seas from pirates were made here. In 1783 it received a commission for the cannons the Spanish Crown used to help the North American settlers win independence from England. It also cast such mighty weapons as 'El Destruidor' (The Destroyer) and 'El Tigre' (The Tiger), a 1797 shot from which took Admiral Nelson's arm clean off at the battle of Santa Cruz de Tenerife; the same Nelson who would later become famous for the Battle of Trafalgar.

WATER RESERVOIR IN JARDINES DE LA BUHAIRA

The orchard of the kings of Al-Andalus

Avenida de la Buhaira, 20
Daily 8am–10pm
Admission free

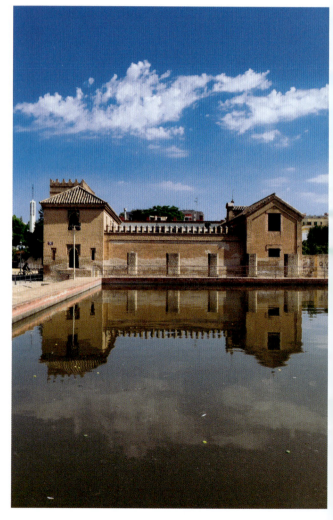

Off the tourist trail, in the neighbourhood known as the Huerta del Rey (King's Orchard), the gardens of La Buhaira are home to the palace and the series of orchards and gardens built in 1171 on the orders of Abu Yaqub Yusuf, the Almohad Caliph of Seville.

The most interesting aspect of the enclosure is the enormous *alberca* (reservoir), measuring some 40 metres long, located next to the palace. It was filled with water from the old Caños de Carmona aqueduct, also rebuilt by the Caliph of Seville (see p. 128). Having powered a number of mills, it collected the water which was then sent along irrigation channels feeding orchards and gardens. The reservoir also served as a leisure and recreation area during the harsh Seville summers.

Since its discovery in 1971, successive archaeological digs have gradually revealed other finds to join the great *alberca*, such as the remains of the old palace, the aqueduct, irrigation channels and the Mudéjar gateway.

After the dilapidated ruins of the old palace were pulled down in the late 19th century, a Mudéjar-style pavilion was erected for the purposes of recalling past splendours. This is currently used as a cultural centre. Alongside that building, the original palace floorplan and the beginning of pillars and walls can be seen.

The old Mudéjar gateway, located in the gardens next to the Artillery Factory, was the main entrance, referred to by the chronicles of the day as that of 'shields and broken swords'. How many battles and violent skirmishes must have taken place there over the centuries?

The project for the palace and gardens was overseen by Ahmed ben Baso, known as 'the chief of those who built in Al-Andalus'. This was the same architect responsible some years later for erecting the great mosque and its minaret, today's Giralda. Its name comes from the great lagoon, Al-Buhayra, which the poet-king Al-Mutamid ordered to be emptied and flattened a century earlier to make way for the construction of a series of leisure rooms and orchards. The surviving chronicles from the period provide ample information on the entire ensemble. The palaces and orchards of Al-Andalus also included residential spaces, walls and surveillance towers, gardens, orchards, olive and citrus groves, irrigation channels and reservoirs. It was here that the expert Moorish agronomists showed off their skills. The garden as a metaphor for paradise as set out in the Koran.

Triana and Los Remedios

LAST VESTIGES OF TRIANA'S REALES ALMONAS

When Seville exported soap to the entire world …

Calle Castilla, 39

Just next to the church of Nuestra Señora de la O, an unassuming porch opens out onto an alley leading down to the banks of the river. This plain little archway is one of the few vestiges of Triana's Reales Almonas (Royal Soap Factories), which produced soap from the 15th century until they closed in the early 20th century, despite being revamped in 1906. A tile at the entrance is a reminder of the importance of this industry, considered 15th-century Seville's foremost capitalist enterprise. If you go down the alley until you reach the embankment you'll see some even older remains on your right: a blind arch and an enormous and strange brick

structure incorporated into the ground floor of the buildings. The *almonas* were the soap factories located in the stretch between the little archway and an alley called the Callejón de la Inquisición. This was where the world-famous Seville soap was made, and these very river banks housed the docks where materials were unloaded for its manufacture. It was from here that the finished product set sail for England, Flanders, the Americas and the entire Mediterranean. Two varieties of soap were manufactured. Firstly, there was a soft dark type made out of potash, but the most highly sought-after variety was hard white soap, which benefited from the innovative use of caustic soda. This gained a reputation for being superior to the soaps produced in the best European factories of Savona (Italy) and Marseille (France). Its manufacture depended on the excellent olive oil produced in Seville's El Aljarafe region, and the caustic soda obtained from the ash of *Salsola kali*, a flowering plant from the amaranth family growing in the nearby marshlands, which was perfumed with musk, amber or mint.

Of Islamic origin, after the Christian conquest the soap factories became Crown property. Towards the end of the 15th century they were granted by royal privilege to the Enríquez de Ribera family, the Dukes of Alcalá, who owned the lavish Renaissance palace known as Casa de Pilatos (see p. 116). They subsequently exchanged their monopoly over the industry in return for a considerable income, first to impresarios of Genovese origin and later

to the Wesler family, responsible for the prestige of the product under the tradename Jabón de Castilla (Castilian Soap). A famous engraving by Simon van der Neuvel (1572) testifies to its importance.

NEARBY
Corral de las flores ②
Calle Castilla, 16

Triana was the Seville district with the greatest number of *corrales de vecinos*, a sort of tenement housing block with modest quarters and a shared inner patio. Built in 1903, this *corral* is one of the oldest in Seville, and also one of the most florid. One curious feature is the communal washing area whose water was supplied by the well next to it. In addition, at the back it has a vantage point looking out over the river.

CERAMIC ADVERT FOR GUADALQUIVIR STEAMBOATS

When the beach started in Triana ...

Restaurante Casa Cuesta
Calle Castilla, 1

LINEA DE VAPORES
SEVILLA-SANLUCAR-MAR

SERVICIO DIARIO ENTRE
SEVILLA Y
LA DESEMBOCADURA DEL
GUADALQUIVIR

On the wall of Casa Cuesta, a restaurant on the Triana district's Calle Castilla, there is a great mosaic of ceramic tiles from the 1920s depicting a paddle steamer ploughing through the waters of the Guadalquivir. From the shore, two cattle herders with their horse and dog take a break from breeding fighting bulls to wave to the steamboat as it races along. In the foreground is the eye-catching banner of the maritime company, a flag with a blue background and red Maltese Cross.

The panel of tiles makes up an attractive piece of advertising for the Sevilla-Sanlúcar-Mar steamboat company, created in 1922 by the Marquis of Olaso. The first boat, and the flagship of the fleet, was the *San Telmo* paddle steamer, which was built in England in 1876 and bought by Luis de Olaso in 1921. This vessel would be joined by other steamboats, the *Bajo de Guía*, *Sanlúcar* and *Cádiz*, all with their red and black-painted chimneys.

They made the 4½-hour trip several times a day all year round, though more often in the summer months, as Sanlúcar (Cádiz) was the Seville beach destination par excellence. The boats included all manner of comfort, such as saloons and dining rooms (first and second class), electric lighting, heating ... and the most luxurious vessel, the *Sanlúcar*, even boasted a restaurant, a ballroom and a reading room.

The steamboat departure station was next to Triana bridge, in a building known as the Triana *faro* (lighthouse), and on arriving at Sanlúcar they moored at the Olaso docks, named after the founder of the steamboat company. It ceased operating in 1932, converting the *San Telmo* into a little floating hotel until it was decommissioned in 1935, drawing the final curtain on a golden age in which it was said that 'the beach started in Triana'.

> Another similar panel of ceramic tiles is found on the front wall of a private residence on the corner of Avenida de América and Calle Martínez de León, in Coria del Río (Seville).

NEARBY

Triana lighthouse: old steamboat station

Next to Triana bridge is a cute little yellow building crowned with a square clock tower. Known as the Faro de Triana (Triana Lighthouse), it was built in 1924 as the steamboat departure station, housing the ticket and admin offices. A little internal stairway on the ground floor led out onto the dock, where you can still see the boats' mooring post. When the company closed down the station lost its function, being put to various uses (seed warehouse, grocer's and so on), and has served as a restaurant since the 1980s.

CENTRO CERÁMICA TRIANA

④

The place where Seville's world-famous ceramics and tiles were made

Calle Callao, 16
Tuesday–Saturday 10am–2pm & 5pm–8pm
Sunday & public holidays 10am–3pm

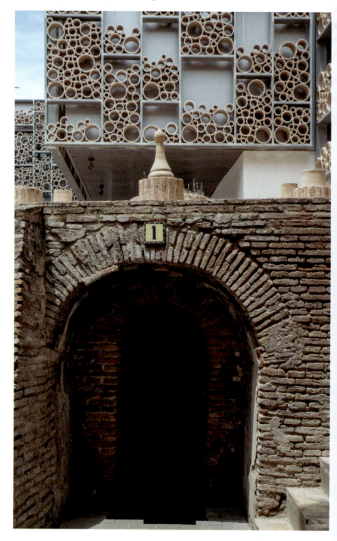

The former Santa Ana factory cannot be seen from the street – it's tucked away behind residential buildings and the occasional business premises. It continued to operate until the late 20th century, so during its renovation and conversion into a Ceramics Centre there were still numerous well-preserved items located in their original context.

With roots going back to the Middle Ages, this ceramics workshop was one of the last centres of production in the city. In its heyday it employed around 50 workers, from those that manned the furnaces to painters, turners and so on, with the trade being passed down through the generations, manufacturing Seville's world-famous ceramics and tiles.

Nowadays, through the maze-like ground floor visitors are introduced to the secrets of Triana's ceramics tradition. This initiation takes in various furnaces for firing ceramics (in addition to the seven that were recovered, another eight were dug up, some dating from the 16th century), the water well, mineral grinders, stores of clays and pigments, the potter's wheel and the wooden work bench on which the painters executed their large panels of tiles.

The permanent collection on the upper level includes major works from Al-Andalus along with others created by Aníbal González to decorate Plaza de España (see p. 250), and others from the Marquis of Pickman, who breathed new life into this industry with his factory in La Cartuja. Finally, there are curious samples of the ceramic advertising that could be found all over the city. Worth highlighting is the work of Niculoso Pisano, who introduced the new Italian approach to ceramics decoration and manufacture in the 16th century, leaving a mark that lives on today.

Ceramics was a major activity that set the Triana district apart for centuries, thanks to its proximity to the river, easy access to raw materials and the arrangement of available spaces far from housing. At its peak, around the time of the 1929 Ibero-American Expo, there were more than 20 active factories.

NEARBY

Calle Alfarería ⑤

The name of this street fits it like a glove, given this was where the majority of Triana's *alfarerías* (ceramics workshops), were located. One of the most prominent of these was Cerámica Montalván at No. 23, first opened in the 19th century and now converted into a hotel where many original pieces of interest have been recovered. Note also that No. 22 is home to the workshop of Antonio Campos, the street's last active potter.

CASALA THEATRE SEATS

The old seats from the Bretón de los Herreros Theatre in Logroño

Plaza del Altozano
Mercado de Triana
Pitches 11 and 12
casalateatro.com

aking up two pitches in Triana market, between stalls selling vegetables, fish and meat, and amidst the hubbub of buyers and sellers, is one of the smallest conventional theatres in the world, measuring just 28 square metres. Along with its reduced size and its location in the middle of a farmers' market (the only one in the world to have a theatre), the oddest thing about this pocket-sized stage is that its 28 seats once belonged to the Bretón de los Herreros Theatre in Logroño, first opened in 1880. The promotors of Casala tracked down the old Bretón seats being used in the Niños Perdidos (Lost Children) theatre school in the same city in the Rioja region. After that centre closed, the seats were taken to Seville in 2012, thereby perpetuating their use in a theatrical setting.

NEARBY
Callejón de la Inquisición ⑦

At the start of the 20th century, this pedestrian alleyway connecting Calle Castilla with Paseo de la O on the banks of the river was given the name Callejón de la Inquisición (Alleyway of the Inquisition). This was because it ran along the side of the Castillo de San Jorge, an old Almohad fortification that was occupied by the Courts of the Holy Inquisition in 1481 (see p. 206). It was pulled down in the 19th century, making way in 1823 for a farmers' market, the predecessor to today's Triana market.

NIGHT WATCHMAN MARCHENA'S WEATHER VANE

Keeping a lookout over the skies of Triana

Capilla del Carmen
Puente de Isabel II

As you pass Triana bridge, just before the market you come across the Capilla del Carmen chapel, built by Aníbal González in 1928. This little building with two parts, chapel and bell tower, was constructed using exposed brickwork and ceramics, and due to its odd shape it was popularly nicknamed '*el mechero*' (the cigarette lighter).

At the top of the bell tower is an iron weather vane featuring a curious figure who has a lantern in one hand and a spiked walking stick in the other. This is Marchena, the night watchman, also known as the *veleta* (weather vane). His is a bizarre story.

Marchena worked as the night watchman in Triana during the reign of Alfonso XII, towards the end of the 19th century. In the early hours one night a fighting bull ran astray and was seen rampaging through the neighbourhood at will, so Marchena decided to warn both residents and passers-by of the danger. Just as he was doing so, he was gored by the animal who, in his own words: 'tossed him up above the rooftops so he could even see the masts of the ships'. In memory of the night watchman, his silhouette flutters with the wind at the top of the bell tower.

Inside the chapel there is a canvas dedicated to Our Lady of Mount Carmel dating back to the 18th century, which was in the original chapel that was on this site when there was a floating or pontoon bridge here. Curiously, nobody seems to realise that the cupola on the top of the chapel houses the figures of the patron saints of the city, St Justa and St Rufina, along with a replica of the Giralda.

NEARBY
The lion's mouth

Opposite the Capilla del Carmen is the Triana lighthouse (see p. 199).

Going down a set of stairs to the right, named Tagua after the man who built them, you arrive at the old dock. There, in a corner of the lighthouse wall, looking out over the river, there is a little white stone sculpture in the shape of a lion's mouth. For centuries it served a really important function, indicating whether there was flooding as the water levels rose. 'Just another handspan and the water will be up to the lion's mouth', locals would say.

SAN JORGE CASTLE'S CENTRO TEMÁTICO DE LA TOLERANCIA

The Inquisition's secret dungeons

Triana farmers' market
Plaza del Altozano (next to Triana bridge)
Monday–Friday 9am–1.30pm & 3.30pm–8pm
Saturday, Sunday & public holidays 10am–2pm
Admission free

When Triana's locals are buying at the market they often forget they are treading on the remains of the fortress that for three centuries housed the shadowy headquarters of the Seville Inquisition.

If you go down the market steps leading to the bridge, on the left you'll see the entrance to the underground tour of the Tolerance Theme Centre in the remains of the castle of San Jorge, a medieval construction of Almohad origin which, from the 15th century onwards, was given over to the trials trying to root out heretics and closet Jews. These remains were discovered in 1990 during building works for the new market.

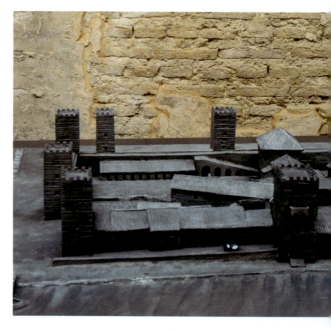

The tour includes archaeological remains such as the caretaker's house, the stables, the houses of the Nuncio and the *notario del secreto*, a sort of secretary appointed to draft trial documents, the hearing room, the house of the first Inquisitor and those of the *familiares*, lay servants of the Inquisition who carried out police work, reporting and arresting heretics. A large-scale model also shows how the castle was more like a real citadel, with buildings and streets, the paving of which has been recovered in perfect condition, and which was the same as the rest of the city in the 17th century.

The Puerta de Barcas gateway has also survived, one of the main entrances leading out onto a dock and the pavement that linked up with the floating or pontoon bridge. Nothing, however, remains of the secret dungeons, divided up into upper and lower cells, each one as damp and insalubrious as the next. Nor is there any trace of the so-called torment room in the tower of San Jerónimo, where Calle Callao runs today.

This is where suspects were subjected to interrogations and tortures that in the best scenarios might lead to the loss of possessions and a prison sentence. Those not so lucky would be marched on procession over the old floating bridge that spanned the Guadalquivir to a public sentencing in an *auto-da-fé* held in Plaza de San Francisco, where the condemned were burned at the stake on the sinister Tablada pyre.

Over the years, the city's collective memory of this gloomy place has faded. Neglect and the damage caused by the continual floods forcing the Inquisitors to leave the complex led to its demolition in 1803, with the Town Council subsequently allowing the plot to be used as a market.

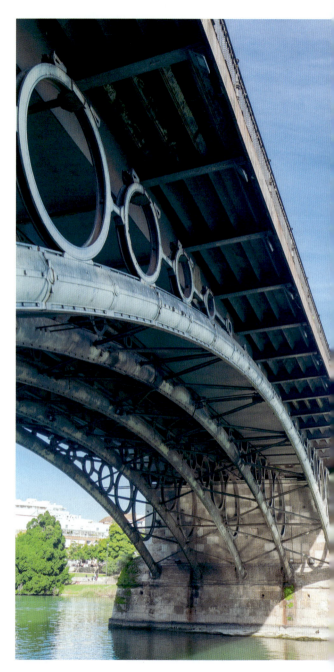

Triana bridge: inspired by the Pont du Carrousel in Paris

Until the 19th century there was no stable or solid connection between the two banks of the Guadalquivir, between the capital and the Triana district and, as such, the fertile Aljarafe region. As incredible as it sounds, the floating bridge first built by the Almohad Caliph Abu Yaqub Yusuf in 1171, made up of boats linked together by iron chains supporting heavy-duty wooden planks, was active for seven centuries. It wasn't until 1852 that work concluded on the current main bridge designed by French engineers Steinacher and Bernadet. This is considered the oldest iron bridge in Spain, and a benchmark of 19th-century industrial architecture. The bridge was christened with the name of Isabella II, during whose reign it was built, though more widely known as Triana bridge. And it was certainly not the work of Eiffel, as has been claimed on occasion, given he was only 12 when work on the bridge began. In fact the model used was the Pont du Carrousel in Paris, the work of the engineer Antoine Rémy Polonceau. His design came up with an innovative arched structure, whose daring approach came in for considerable criticism, even winning it the ironic nickname 'napkin ring' bridge. The Paris bridge was demolished in 1930, a hundred years after it was built, due to its low clearance height making river navigation difficult, and was subsequently replaced by another bridge.

It seems that the choice of this model for Seville was due to the great interest shown by the Duke and Duchess of Montpensier, who knew the bridge over the Seine. In fact, Duke Antoine d'Orléans, the son of the French King Louis Philippe I, was the one who opened the Pont du Carrousel in 1834. Triana bridge presents three equal spans, supported on two central pillars, and all the cast ironwork was carried out at the Narciso Bonaplata foundry in Seville. The bridge underwent all sorts of modifications and renovations right from the outset, largely due to the increase in motorised traffic. When a self-supporting metal slab was installed in 1977, the iron arches lost their function, remaining solely as decorative features, one of the city's most iconic images.

FARMACIA MURILLO CERAMICS

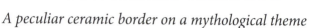

A peculiar ceramic border on a mythological theme

Plaza del Altozano, 12
Monday–Friday 9.30am–2pm & 5pm–8pm, Saturday 9.30am–2pm

The Murillo family chemist's in Triana was built in 1913 as designed by architect José Espiau, who gave it a façade in a Regionalist style, made from brick and ceramics with lobed arches.

It retains all its 19th-century charm, including the original shelves with decorated ceramic pots featuring the company logo.

Of a total of 195 pieces from the late 19th century and the first quarter of the 20th century, some are from Germany, though the majority are works of opaque china porcelain from the Pickman factory in La Cartuja (see p. 276) and earthenware cups from Cerámica Montalván in Triana.

Behind the red marble counter used for serving the public, and through a carved wooden arch, you reach the back room where the chemist mixed his medicines.

Of particular note are the impressive ceramic borders by ceramicist Vigil Escalera, depicting mythological subjects.

The one on the left portrays Theseus, the mythological Athenian hero who killed the Minotaur in the Cretan labyrinth, symbolising victory over illness.

The one on the right, meanwhile, features the figure of Asclepius, the god of Medicine, accompanied by his daughters, Iaso and Panacea.

Theseus also lent his name to the laboratory that used to be attached to the chemist's, whose logo featured the Greek hero inside a triangle made up of three words: science, conscience and patience.

The pharmacy is currently being run by the fourth generation in this dynasty of chemists, which started when Francisco Murillo Hernández settled in the city, having come from Vélez-Málaga.

In addition to this age-old apothecary, the family also had another chemist's in Plaza del Salvador, whose utensils and original Cuban mahogany furniture carved with motifs alluding to the pharmaceutical profession are on display today in the Museo de Historia de la Farmacia (see p. 266).

REMAINS OF THE HISPANO AVIACIÓN FACTORY

Commemorating a warplane factory

Calle San Jacinto, 102-106

On Triana's Calle San Jacinto there is a modernist façade featuring a relief of the winged helmet of Mercury, the fleet-footed god of trade, flanked by cornucopias, symbol of plenty, framing an inscription with the date 1918. The year refers to the founding of the iron and timber warehouses which the Hispano-Suiza company took over in

1937, towards the start of the Spanish Civil War, the first Spanish factory to build a jet plane.

The façade from that factory still survives today, along with a hangar converted into a gym and a number of manufacturing buildings that were reconverted in 1990.

The factory was initially given over to repairing the planes of the rebels and, when the war was over, it was semi-nationalised and renamed Hispano Aviación. In 1943, while the Second World War raged, it bought a licence to manufacture the iconic Nazi fighter aircraft the Messerschmitt BF 109, backbone of the Luftwaffe. These planes were named after their designer, engineer Willy Messerschmitt who, following some years of imprisonment after the war had ended, finally found refuge in Spain.

In 1951, following the signing of an agreement to develop the HA-200 Saeta Mach 2 jet plane, Messerschmitt was officially named as director of Hispano Aviación's design department, building up a team including the crème de la crème of Spanish aeronautical engineers and technicians of the day. The German engineer would remain in Spain until 1959 when he returned to Germany, though he maintained a financial stake in Spanish aeronautics through his own companies.

By the time the factory closed down in 1972 it had built a total of 604 aircraft. It was subsequently sold to Egypt, where the facilities and the majority of the equipment were soon destroyed by Israel.

Seville is currently a major centre of the European aeronautics industry thanks to the Airbus A400 assembly plant.

The mystery of the Triana 'Negro'

Church of Santa Ana
Calle Pelay Correa
Monday–Friday 10.30am–1.30pm
Tuesday & Wednesday 1 October–15 June 4.30pm–6.30pm

The Triana district's church of Santa Ana, the oldest house of worship in Seville, conceals a secret that has survived the passing years.

On the right-hand side of the Epistle nave is the most beautiful ceramic tombstone commemorating a mysterious character called Iñigo López. The restoration work of 2016 returned the piece to all its original splendour, depicting a man holding a cross, wearing a greenish-ochre cloak, blue cap, green tights and black shoes, and his head resting on a sumptuous, embroidered pillow.

The border of the tombstone, which runs around the effigy of the deceased, features a signature and the year the work was executed: *Niculoso Francisco italiano me fecit en el agno de MILCCCCCIII* (Niculoso Francisco the Italian made me in 1503), indicating that this was the first recorded work carried out in Seville by the renowned ceramicist Niculoso Pisano (Pisa, 1470–Seville, 1529). Pisano revolutionised ceramic techniques, successfully painting polychrome motifs on flat tiles as if they were canvases, without fear of the colours bleeding into each other during firing as had previously been the case.

This tomb remained hidden for centuries, and it wasn't until 1844 that it was found behind an altarpiece to St Cecilia during building works. For reasons that remain something of a mystery, a rumour quickly circulated that if a single woman kicked the effigy of the deceased man seven times she would find a husband, and even fall pregnant. This legend became so popular that a railing had to be erected to save the tomb from further damage. Fortunately, restoration work has recovered the deceased man's features, which had faded under the constant barrage of kicks received from Triana women over the years.

The enigma surrounding this figure only increased when it was discovered that someone had deliberately rubbed out his second surname, title and profession.

According to popular legend, Iñigo López was a slave in the service of a marquis, although it's certainly odd to see a slave buried dressed as a noble under an extremely valuable Renaissance ceramic tombstone. Some versions of the story call him 'El Negro', claiming he was a Caribbean Indian brought back to Seville by Columbus himself, and who died a violent death on refusing to have relations with his master.

NEARBY

Cervantine tile on the wall of Casa de Monipodio ⑬
Calle Betis, 69

The tile erected in 1916 on the wall looking over Calle Troya is a reminder that the location of this 18th-century *corral de vecinos* (tenement block) was used by Cervantes for the house of Monipodio, the head of the Seville 'guild' of rogues and scoundrels.

EARTH'S MILE ZERO MONUMENT ⑭

The place where the first circumnavigation of the globe started and finished

Plaza de Cuba, next to Calle Juan Sebastián Elcano

Also known as an 'armillary sphere', the Milla Cero de la Tierra (Earth's Mile Zero) monument is in Plaza de Cuba, just on the corner of Calle Juan Sebastián Elcano and opposite the Guadalquivir. First unveiled in 2010, the monument consists of a steel armillary sphere 3.5 metres across standing on the site of the old Las Muelas dock, the place from which the fleet sailed on the first circumnavigation of the globe. The monument draws inspiration from the design of the armillary sphere that appears on the cover of Fernández de Enciso's book *Suma de Geographia*, printed in 1519 in the workshop of the German printer Cromberger (see p. 96). Our planet is arranged in the centre,

depicted as a ball surrounded by rings or bracelets (*armilla* in Latin) to represent the horizon, equator, zodiacal band, the tropics and so on.

The sphere represents a reduced model of the cosmos used in astronomy and navigation to establish the coordinates of celestial bodies (stars, planets, satellites). Following the formulation of Copernicus' heliocentric model in 1543, armillary spheres' structures were modified to include the Sun at the centre.

The expedition made up of five ships and 243 men set sail under the command of Ferdinand Magellan on 10 August 1519, with the goal of reaching the Spice Islands (Maluku Islands in today's Indonesia). Three years later, on 8 September 1522, Juan Sebastián Elcano would return with just one ship, *Santa María de la Victoria*, and a crew of 17. Having undergone all sorts of hardships, they managed to complete the first ever circumnavigation of the globe. The day after their arrival in Seville the 18 survivors, stripped down to their shirtsleeves, barefoot and holding votive candles in their hands, fulfilled their promise to visit the images of Nuestra Señora de la Victoria (Our Lady of Victory) and Santa María la Antigua (St Mary the Ancient). In recognition of his astonishing achievement, Emperor Charles V awarded Elcano a considerable annual pension and a coat of arms featuring a globe with the motto *Primus circumdedisti me*, meaning 'You were the first to go around me', where can also be seen three nutmegs, two sticks of cinnamon and twelve cloves, referring to the spices the expedition brought back.

NEARBY

Instituto Hispano-Cubano ⑮

Juan Sebastián Elcano, 2
954 273 602
institutohispanocubano.org
Tuesday–Thursday 10am–1pm, admission free

The Instituto Hispano-Cubano de Historia de América (Hispano-Cuban Institute for the History of the Americas) is located in the old 17th-century convent of the Discalced Carmelites, renovated in 1928 by the Regionalist architect Juan Talavera. The convent, which was dedicated to Our Lady of the Remedies, was built on the site of a little chapel given over to said Marian title, to whom sailors would commend themselves before embarking for the Americas. In fact, the Las Muelas dock at the foot of the convent witnessed the departure of both Magellan and Elcano on the first journey around the world, as is commemorated by the 1919 plaque on the side wall. The institute currently boasts a major library specialising in Americanist subjects.

BARBERÍA MUSEUM

A decidedly odd barber's shop

Calle Virgen del Valle, 95
Monday–Friday 10am–1.30pm & 5.30pm–8.30pm
Saturday 10am–1.30pm

Just over the river and next to Triana is the Los Remedios district, with its abundance of streets named after either the Virgin Mary or a host of odd characters. One of the latter was Seville's rocker par excellence, Silvio Fernández Melgarejo. Something of an outcast during his lifetime, he was awarded the medal of the city after his death in 2001 and had a street in the neighbourhood where he lived named after him: Calle Rockero Silvio. Not far from here, in another Virgin-inspired street, you can visit the secular shrine to Seville's rock tradition and the martyr of both street and bar life that was Silvio: the Barber's Museum.

The hairdresser's was founded in the early 1980s by Curro Silver Barber (Seville, 1944), and is now run by his son.

Curro used to make the distinction between the words *pelos* and *cabellos*, which both mean hair, though the latter is far more elegant. As he used to say: '*pelos* are used by animals for their own protection, what we do here is cut and style people's *cabellos*'. Stacked to the rafters with memorabilia, a mishmash of oddities and gifts from friends, the barber's shop presents an ordered chaos of photos, figurines, old cameras, records and projectors littering the walls, corners and even the ceiling.

Customers who enter here are taking a trip back to the 1960s as they recline in any one of the three perfectly preserved green Eurostyle leather retro barber's chairs. Above the mirror is the motto of this bizarre establishment: *Tijeras de plata para un público de oro* (Silver scissors for a gilt-edged clientele).

Don Curro was one of the precursors of Seville rock. In addition to playing the guitar, he also made his own instruments. A huge fan of The Shadows, on putting down his scissors at the end of the day he would often plug in his guitar and listen to it wail through the 17 speakers concealed around the shop. Silvio, a friend with whom he shared many a stage during their early days together, takes pride of place here among all the treasured memorabilia. Portraits, photos, records, press cuttings, posters ... and the medal awarded for merit as a rocker. They all bear witness to an uncategorisable Seville musician who mixed rock and Italian *canzone* with the music of the city's Holy Week.

On the street door, among posters and advertising slogans born of the artist's imagination, such as *Bienvenido al edén del cabello* (Welcome to Hair Eden), there is a sign reading 'Penny Lane'. This refers to the fact that the barber's museum is twinned with the most famous of Liverpudlian barber's shops to which The Beatles dedicated their song.

Puerta de Jerez
and Avenida de la Palmera

MUSEO MARÍTIMO DE LA TORRE DEL ORO

A secluded and little-known museum of Seville and the sea

Paseo Cristóbal Colón
954 22 24 19
torreoro@fn.mde.es
Monday–Friday 9.30am–7pm, Saturday and Sunday 10.30am–7pm
Monday: free admission

The Torre del Oro (Golden Tower) houses a small yet fascinating museum focusing on how important Seville once was in the maritime world. The museum, still unknown to most Seville locals, is arranged over the two floors of the Almohad tower that are open to the public, and includes a panoramic terrace which was once used by sentries looking out for possible river attacks on the city.

The first floor provides a review of the history of the tower up to the point when the Casa de Contratación (House of Trade), which managed all trade relations with the Americas, moved from Seville to Cádiz in 1717. The second floor offers an exhibition covering varying periods of Spanish naval history, displaying maps, nautical charts, paintings and engravings of marine subjects, navigation instruments, historical documents and so on.

The museum in a tower – erected in 1221 to complete the Almohad city's defences – has been managed by the Spanish Ministry of Defence since it was first opened in 1944. Prior to that the tower housed the Marine Command Headquarters and Port Authorities, and before that it had served as prison, housing, chapel and even gunpowder depot.

Legends behind the origin of the tower name

Many tales have been told about the origin of the 'Golden Tower' name, with one claiming it was once covered in golden tiles, another that it was close to the Islamic mint, or alternatively that it was the customs house where all the gold arriving from the Americas was stored. The real explanation is far more prosaic. During restoration works its famously shiny appearance was discovered to be due to a mortar mix containing lime and straw which had been used to plaster the watchtower. Another myth involving the building claimed it was connected to the Triana side of the river by a chain, but what the chain actually did was link the pontoon bridge's boats to the two banks.

NEARBY

Mirrors onto the river

Opposite the Torre del Oro, on the corner of Paseo de Cristóbal Colón, there are two big bronze plaques on the base of a building designed by architect Rafael Moneo in 1987 for the Previsión Española insurance company, showing what this part of the river was like in 1883. One plaque has an image of the Torre del Oro and boats on the Guadalquivir, while the other depicts the palace of San Telmo from the same period.

TORRE DE LA PLATA

The neglected little sister

Calle Santander, 15
Walkway open daily 10am–10pm, with access to foot of tower

The Torre de la Plata (Silver Tower) is the best-kept secret of Seville monuments. Compared with the way the Torre del Oro has been pampered over the years, its little sister has been neglected and, often enough, mistreated, surviving hidden within a maze of buildings and a car park. With its octagonal footprint, it was joined to the Real Alcázar and Torre del Oro by a stretch of city wall which served to protect the port area until it was demolished in 1821. There is a degree of controversy surrounding its origin; some historians argue it was built in the 13th century during the Almohad period, while others claim it dates from after the Christian conquest. Its name probably derives from the whiteness of the lime mortar with which its walls were plastered. During the reign of Alfonso X it was also known as the Torre de los Azacanes (Tower of the Water Carriers) because it was next to the little entrance of the same name used by water carriers. This entrance, which was one of the main gateways linking up with the port, was subsequently known as the Postigo del Carbón (Coal Gate) due to the influx of said commodity.

Over time, the tower was absorbed into the Casa de la Moneda (Mint, see below) complex, and subsequently went on to have numerous functions, such as gunpowder and weapons depot as well as housing. Renovated in 1992, it now serves as the headquarters of the Seville Town Council heritage services.

NEARBY

Casa de la Moneda ③

Calle Habana

Just off Calle Habana an arched inner patio marks the site where Philip II ordered the Mint factory merchants' square to be built in 1584. The main façade balcony has also survived from a complex that once housed furnaces, workshops, warehouses, offices and living space, and which covered the entire process from delivery of the metals (hence its proximity to the river) to the casting, carving, cutting, cleaning and selling. Seville started receiving a deluge of precious metals in the early 16th century. This was the gold and silver brought on the galleons arriving from the New World when the city was granted a monopoly over trade with the Americas in 1503 – the reason behind the building of this factory. Its current structure is due to the renovation works undertaken following the Lisbon earthquake of 1755, including the main entrance into Calle Santander and the Fundición Real (Royal Foundry), now home to a theatre. The life of this Seville factory came to a close in 1869 when it was sold and converted into residential property. Its inner streetways were rechristened by the new owners, who had made their fortune in Cuba, with the names of towns on the Caribbean island: Habana, Güiñes, San Nicolás and El Jobo.

TORRE DE ABDELAZIZ

*A medieval watchtower camouflaged among
Regionalist-style buildings*

Avenida de la Constitución, 15

Between Avenida de la Constitución and Calle Santo Tomás a little hexagonal tower is tucked away, camouflaged between buildings that dwarf it, leaving only four of its six walls free, each one measuring 1.5 metres.

A range of materials were used in the construction of the 15-metre Tower of Abdelaziz, such as rammed earth, brick, and stone blocks at the corners.

It appears to have been erected during the reforms to the Alcázar complex undertaken in the reign of Peter I in the 14th century, along with the nearby Arquillo de la Victoria/Plata, also in a Mudéjar style. It may also have been built on the site of a previous *atalaya* (watchtower), part of the Almohad Alcázar built in the 12th century which collapsed in the 1356 earthquake.

The tower has been given a long list of names: 'de Abdelaziz', 'del Homenaje' and, most recently, 'de Santo Tomás', due to its location in the street named after the doubting saint.

The tradition goes that the original tower was the first to raise Ferdinand III's standard when he conquered Seville in 1248, an act of homage that won it the '*del homenaje*' epithet. Legend has it that the historic banner, now housed in the cathedral, was hoisted by Scottish knights involved in the siege of the city.

Finally, the Tower of Abdelaziz was named in honour of Abd al-Aziz ibn Musa, the second *wali* (governor) of Al-Andalus, who lived in Seville (Isbilya) where he married Egilon, widow of King Roderic. Abd al-Aziz arrived along with his father in 712 for the conquest of the Visigothic Kingdom of Hispania, and within two years they had reached Lérida, Lugo and Porto. In 716 he was murdered on the orders of Caliph Sulayman I, and his head was sent to Damascus.

NEARBY
Torre del Bronce (5)

Calle Santander, 1

During a 2012 restoration of a building in order to convert it into a restaurant, workers were surprised to uncover an Almohad tower with a square floorplan. The original edifice was Casa del Tesorero (House of the Treasurer), home to the royal official in charge of the Casa de la Moneda or Mint (see p. 225). Dated to around the late 11th or early 12th centuries, the Torre del Bronce (Bronze Tower) was part of the Alcázar wall extension undertaken to defend the city from possible invaders coming up the river, taking in the Torre de la Plata and culminating with the Torre del Oro.

STONE PLAQUE
OF THE PUERTA DE JEREZ

Sole reminder of a gateway demolished in 1864

Corner of Calle Maese Rodrigo de Sevilla and Avenida de la Constitución

The long-lost Puerta de Jerez was one of the four main gateways to the city as early as the Middle Ages, controlling the movements of both people and carriages heading south towards Jerez from the 15th century onwards. Hence its name. In the most unlikely of places (look up towards the top of the building in the corner of Calle Maese Rodrigo), the sole surviving reminder of this gateway is a marble plaque with an inscription that would have presided over the arch.

As may be seen, this plaque, which was renovated in 1622, summarises the history of Seville: 'Hercules built me / Julius Caesar enclosed me / with walls and high towers / the Saint King won me / with Garci Pérez de Vargas ...' The text refers to the mythical founders of Seville, Hercules and Julius Caesar, the latter being quaestor of Hispalis (Seville) in 65 BCE when he may have been responsible for building the Roman city walls,

and Ferdinand III, who conquered the city in the 13th century. According to legend, the king entered through this gateway in disguise, in order to spy on the Islamic defenders before storming the city.

Built in the 12th century by the Almohads, the gateway underwent continual restoration work over the years while maintaining its structure; a gateway flanked by two impressive towers protected by an outer wall and featuring an imposing portcullis. It linked up with the bridge over the Tagarete stream which flowed into the Guadalquivir alongside the Torre del Oro, running along where Calle San Fernando is today. Being the gateway to the outer *alcazaba* (fortress), and one of the most importance entrances, it was open under armed guard 24 hours a day. It began to fall into disrepair in the 19th century and finally disappeared altogether. As such, in 1836 the towers and portcullis were removed, and 10 years later the entire building was demolished, along with the section of wall, being replaced by a monumental gate in a neo-classical style with an archway flanked by two pairs of Tuscan pillars. But that brand-spanking entrance wouldn't last long, and in 1864 it was pulled down as part of the city's new urban planning works. The present-day square was created to mark the 1929 Ibero-American Expo, which involved the removal of the last remaining buildings that had survived the demolition of the gateway. If you want to pinpoint the Puerta's exact location nowadays, you need to stand opposite the right-hand corner of Hotel Alfonso XIII.

Gateways of Seville

Of the 20 or so gateways (*puertas*) and secondary entrances (*postigos*) the Seville city wall once had, only three remain: the Arco de la Macarena, the Puerta de Córdoba and the Postigo de Aceite. To these should also be added the Arco de la Plata (or Puerta de la Victoria) where Calle Miguel Mañara meets Avenida de la Constitución, though this wasn't a gateway in the city wall but an entrance to the Alcázar. Its current conformation is Gothic, and the man behind its 1561 renovation was Hernán Ruiz II, the master builder and architect of the cathedrals of Seville and Córdoba as well as Seville's town hall.

CHAPEL OF SANTA MARÍA DE JESÚS

The last vestiges of Seville's first university

Avenida de la Constitución, 27
Puerta de Jerez
Monday, Tuesday, Wednesday & Friday noon–1.30pm

Located close to the Puerta de Jerez, the chapel of Santa María de Jesús is the last remaining trace of the city's first university, the College/University founded by Canon Maese Rodrigo Fernández de Santaella at the dawn of the 16th century.

The rest of the building was demolished in 1909 to make way for what is now Avenida de la Constitución, and its main stone façade was moved to the grounds of the convent of Santa Clara.

The chapel, completed in 1506, is of a late Gothic-Mudéjar style with a single nave that would originally have been entirely covered in lime plaster. It is crowned by battlements in Omayyad style and an original 16th-century bell gable.

The building presents a spectacular Gothic window with archivolts, and its wall also features a marble plaque referring to the founding of the college. An interesting Gothic gargoyle depicting a dragon stands watch over the wall to the rear.

The entrance is through a two-coloured brick portico covered by an ogee arch, a rare sight in Seville. Highlighted inside, in addition to a beautiful wooden gabled Mudéjar ceiling and impressive Renaissance tile borders, is the altarpiece designed in 1520 in a late Gothic style by Alejo Fernández, painter of various images on the cathedral's main altarpiece.

One notable curiosity is how the Virgin of Antiquity is seen receiving a model of the college building from the hands of its founder, whose tomb lies at the foot of the retablo, under the altar.

Maese Rodrigo, a learned man who studied in Bologna (Italy), and from what appears to have been a Jewish *converso* family, purchased the original site in an area known as the 'Corral de Jerez', where the last Jews in the city had settled prior to their final expulsion. Although he received a papal bull in 1508 allowing for classes in the same subjects taught at the University of Salamanca, including the Arts, Logic, Philosophy, Theology, Law and Medicine, it wasn't until 10 years later, when the rest of the university building was completed, that the college statutes were approved and the first students were invited to enrol.

CALZADA ROMANA

The forgotten paths of Baetica

Avenida de Roma

E verybody walks on them, but very few realise that the huge paving slabs on the pavement next to Hotel Alfonso XIII and the Puerta de Jerez were once part of the Roman road (*calzada*).

These remains were discovered along with a number of major finds from varying periods during building work on an underground car park. Due to its size, almost 5 metres wide, and the dimensions of some of the slabs, more than 50 cm thick, it was concluded it had to be a major thoroughfare.

It seems that this highway linked up with the Via Augusta on its way to Gades (Cádiz). In fact, this was a port area with a great amount of economic activity related to river trade and traffic, and some major shipyards which enjoyed a boom under Emperor Augustus in around the 1st century CE. This is borne out by some valuable mosaics found alongside kilns used to make amphorae for storing oil and wine. Two of these kilns may be visited on the second floor of the car park.

Via Augusta, Baetica's Roman highway

In addition to the river Betis (Guadalquivir), the natural route for moving people and merchandise across the interior of the province of Baetica, the Roman empire also prioritised the importance of having a road network, strategic to military movements, trade, bureaucracy and postal services. The Via Augusta was the main Roman road in Hispania, and in Baetica it ran from east to west, from the Janus Augustus Arch (near Cástulo, Jaén) to Cádiz, linking the capitals of the four *conventus iuridici* in the southern Roman province: Corduba (Córdoba), Astigi (Écija), Hispalis (Seville) and Gades (Cádiz). Having arrived at the last of these cities, travellers could continue to the world-famous Phoenician shrine of Melqart, linked to Hercules, and the isle of Sancti Petri, and leave votive offerings alongside those of figures including Hannibal and Julius Caesar, or admire relics such as the draecana (dragon tree) born of the blood of the giant Geryon, the golden olive tree of Pygmalion and the two metal pillars marking the entrance to the temple itself.

Milestones

In the archaeological museum there is a marble mile marker dedicated to Emperor Hadrian, discovered in the theatre of Italica (Santiponce). These stone steles indicated the distance in miles (*milia passuum*, 1,000 paces or approximately 1,481 metres) to the city or major stopping point, along with the name of the emperor. The earliest guides and roadmaps were made during the Holy Roman Empire and could be bought at markets.

GALLERY OF THE 12 ILLUSTRIOUS SONS OF THE CITY

The last work by sculptor Antonio Susillo

Palacio de San Telmo
Calle Palos de la Frontera

Standing over the balustrade high above the carriage entrance at the front of the palace of San Telmo there is a row of 12 sculptures making up a gallery of illustrious sons of the city, commissioned from sculptor Antonio Susillo in 1895.

Not all the figures from this secular shrine were actually born in Seville, in some cases they simply pursued their careers and died in the city.

Starting from the right, the first member of the gallery is Juan Martínez Montañés, the great Baroque sculptor and a central figure in religious imagery in the city, followed by Rodrigo Ponce de León, the Count of Arcos de la Frontera and one of the major captains in the war against the Kingdom of Granada, who fought alongside the Catholic monarchs.

Next up you come to painter Diego de Velázquez, then Miguel Mañara, the philanthropic monk who founded the Hospital de la Caridad, Lope de Rueda, a seminal figure from Renaissance Spanish theatre and Diego Ortiz de Zúñiga, the city's historical chronicler.

Further along is Fernando de Herrera, the Golden Age poet, Luis Daoíz, one of the heroes of the Peninsula War who died in Madrid on 2 May, Benito Arias Montano, the Seville-born humanist and theologian, Bartolomé Esteban Murillo, the Baroque painter who was a key figure in the Seville school of art, Fernando Afán de Ribera y Enríquez, a politician and humanist who became the Viceroy of Naples and, finally, Bartolomé de las Casas, the chronicler and theologian best known as the 'defender of the Indians'.

The sculptor behind many of the city's major monuments, Susillo used a new and ground-breaking material for this project: cement. As an artist, he broke away from the prevailing Baroque tradition and, from his time studying in Paris where he coincided with Rodin, he introduced work that was markedly influenced by French art.

This sculptural group, a commission from the Duke of Montpensier Antoine d'Orléans and his wife Maria Luis Fernanda, the youngest daughter of Ferdinand VII, would be the last work Susillo saw before he died. The poet-sculptor suffered from delicate mental health aggravated by an unhappy second marriage and the recent deaths of his mother and sister. Plunged into a heavy depression he committed suicide on 22 December 1896 aged just 41, dying by a pistol shot under the chin.

His remains lie at rest in Seville cemetery in a pantheon presided over by his work *Cristo de las Mieles* (see p. 294).

MARITIME SYMBOLS ON THE ENTRANCE TO THE PALACE OF SAN TELMO

Recalling the Universidad de Mareantes

Avenida de Roma, s/n
95 500 1010
juntadeandalucia.es/presidencia/santelmoabierto

S ome will tell you that the great Baroque building erected on the banks of the Guadalquivir at the end of the 17th century, and which currently serves as the headquarters of the Presidential offices of the Junta de Andalucía (Regional Government of Andalusia), was once the residence of the Duke and Duchess of Montpensier. But very few know that prior to that it was the San Telmo Royal Seminary College of the University of 'Mareantes' (Seafarers), founded for the purposes of educating orphans or defenceless children, as well as those of sailors, in the art of navigation, preparing them to be future officers, bosuns and able-bodied seamen in the fleets sailing overseas to the Americas.

The iconography of its impressive main façade entrance recalls this historical function. Firstly, the main balcony is supported by four Atlantes: Native Americans wearing quivers and feather headdresses, highlighting the major role played by the College in the history of the West Indies. The most illuminating element is the group of 12 allegorical female figures in the middle section of the entrance, six on each side of the balcony. They inform students of the centre's educational syllabus, representing the science and arts subjects taught to the future sailors: Astronomy, Geography, Nautical Arts, Chronology, Geometry, Painting, Trigonometry, Arithmetic, Mathematics, Architecture, Sculpture and Music. Over the main balcony is a medallion with the effigy of Philip V, the monarch on the Spanish throne at the time the entrance was completed in 1734, depicted against a background made up of sails and boat rigging with an armillary sphere and holding a rolled-up nautical chart. Finally, in the upper section is the eye-catching figure of San Telmo (St Elmo), the patron saint of sailors and the college, who is holding a boat and a navigation chart, flanked by the patron saints of the city, St Ferdinand and St Hermenegild, referring to the king's support for the architectural project. This entire complex sculptural ensemble carved in stone was the work of the great architect Leonardo de Figueroa and his son Matías, also responsible for the main patio and the church.

For the 160 years of its existence, the college of the University of 'Mareantes' taught more than 3,500 young students, from when it was founded by royal command in 1681 until the institution's move to Malaga in 1841.

You can see the inside of the palace on a guided tour, by appointment, on Thursdays and Saturdays (book online). The palace chapel is particularly interesting, with its main altarpiece dedicated to Our Lady of Bonaria (Fair Winds), to whom sailors commended themselves, the origin of the name of the capital of Argentina.

RELIEF OF AN INDIGENOUS INDIAN SMOKING A PIPE

Tobacco by royal decree

Universidad de Sevilla
Calle San Fernando, 4

The magnificent entrance to the central offices of the University of Seville is decorated with a surprising repertory of reliefs featuring motifs relating to the Americas, such as busts of Christopher Columbus and Hernán Cortés, several ships and, in particular, an indigenous Indian smoking a pipe, commemorating the fact that the building was originally the Royal Tobacco Factory, built in 1758. As soon as the New World was discovered, Seville became one of the main entry points for ships arriving with all sorts of riches, including tobacco. The plant was championed by Seville botanist Nicolás Monardes in the 16th century, and it quickly shared in the European fervour already enjoyed by coffee and chocolate. In 1636 a royal decree granted the city a monopoly over the production

and distribution of tobacco, an activity that underwent a tremendous boom and led to the construction of this building, near the river and with good connections to the royal highways. The place chosen was known as the *Sitio de las calaveras* (Place of the Skulls) on account of burial sites from the Roman era being found there. Built mainly by military engineer Sebastián van der Borcht, the enormous factory had an unmistakeable martial air about it, surrounded by an impressive trench and with lookout posts around the perimeter, manned at all times by soldiers from the Dragoons corps.

When the university lecturers are imprisoned ...

The factory was flanked by two small buildings: on the left a chapel for factory machinists and on the right the complex's prison.

The cells now serve as the university teaching staff offices, and these still bear the original numbered ceramic plaques.

The Royal Tobacco Factory even had its own jurisdiction, with guards in charge of monitoring any crimes committed within its walls, most commonly theft and fraud, as well as its own court, which could pass sentences ranging from temporary loss of freedom to dismissal.

Cigar-makers of Seville: inspiration for Mérimée and Bizet's Carmen

A key moment in the history of the factory was when it started to employ women in 1813. Female workers became a dominant force, numbering as many as 6,000. They were financially independent and often single mothers. They also had strong union representation, leading to numerous riots in the 19th century, demanding their rights and complaining about the mechanisation of their work. Their global fame inspired the character Carmen from Mérimée's 1845 novel of the same name, and Bizet's opera, which premiered in Seville in 1881.

CIGARRERAS AU TRAVAIL (FÁBRICA DE TABACOS DE SÉVILLE).

PILLARS IN THE GARDENS OF THE CHILEAN PAVILION

The last vestiges of the synagogue of Santa Cruz

Calle La Rábida, s/n

F our towering pillars support the high railings of the gardens of the Chilean Pavilion from the Ibero-American Expo of 1929. These columns, similar to those surrounding the cathedral, are made from dark granite, around 3 metres tall and half a metre across.

Largely unknown to locals, they once supported the arches of the since-disappeared medieval synagogue of Santa Cruz, which stood in the square that now bears its name.

Seville's Jewish quarter (*judería*), had three major synagogues, each one founded on the site of mosques granted to the community by Alfonso X once he conquered the city in the 13th century. After the 1391 attacks on the *judería* fuelled by the Archdean of Écija, which led to the deaths of hundreds of Jews, two of these synagogues were converted into churches, adopting the names Santa Cruz and Santa María de las Nieves. According to parish records, the last rabbi of the Santa Cruz synagogue was the renowned Talmudist Yehudá Alobas. At some point after 1482 the last synagogue would also be converted into a church, with the name of San Bartolomé.

In 1810, its ruined state led to the demolition of the synagogue converted into the church of Santa Cruz by the French occupiers. This also meant removing the mortal remains of painter Bartolomé Esteban Murillo, who was buried there, as indicated by a plaque on the west side of the square at the former site of the church.

Nothing remains of the synagogue other than the pillars taken away in 1830 to decorate a botanical garden (never completed) at the palace of San Telmo, at the behest of the Duke of Montpensier, Antoine d'Orléans. Later, part of the palace gardens was used for the 1929 Expo, at which point the road was built where one of the few vestiges of Seville's *judería* still stands, unmoved by the passing years.

For more on the synagogues of the Jewish quarter, see p. 178.

GODDESS OF THE PERUVIAN PAVILION FROM THE 1929 EXPO

Where the Inca lives on

Casa de la Ciencia
Avenida de María Luisa
954 23 23 49
casadelaciencia.csic.es
info.casadelaciencia@csic.es
Tuesday–Sunday 10am–9pm

With its back to the Lope de Vega theatre, the pavilion that Peru built for its participation in the 1929 Ibero-American Expo rises up like a temple in an Incan city.

The most iconic part of the building, shared today by the headquarters of the Peruvian consulate and the Casa de la Ciencia (Science Museum), is reached by crossing the inner patio and climbing the main stairway. The *sanctum sanctorum* is presided over by an allegorical female figure symbolising a mixed-race motherland, a goddess with two protective jaguars watched over by a condor flying above. All of this was the work of the pavilion's architect who used his own wife as a model. The goddess is being honoured by two kneeling statues representing the Spanish conquistador and an indigenous woman, a *ñusta* – the Quechuan word for the princesses in the Incan empire. If you look at the goddess' hands it seems as though something is missing. Studies carried out on the preparatory sketches for the work have discovered that the left hand was holding a staff with the symbol of the shining Sun (Inti).

The design and management of the pavilion building works fell to an architect born in Lucena (Córdoba), Manuel Piqueras Cotolí. Just 10 years earlier he had travelled to Peru after being hired to teach sculpture at the recently founded Escuela Nacional de Bellas Artes in Lima, and while there he forged a new artistic vision, a style named neo-Peruvian, which was a fusion of Spanish heritage with a major influence of pre-Hispanic motifs.

This approach is also seen in the entrance to the pavilion, dedicated to Viracocha, the principal Incan deity, creator of both the visible and invisible, the main figure at the front depicted holding on to two serpents as if they were staffs. Underneath is the coat of arms of Peru with two heraldic motifs referring to the coat of arms of the Spanish conquistador (Charles V) and the Incan warrior (Manco Cápac). Notable features on the outside of the building are the impressive rows of mahogany balconies, so typical of Lima.

The magnificent central patio is surrounded by arches also decorated with motifs from Incan and pre-Incan cultures, with sculptures and reliefs depicting the country's wildlife (monkey, llama, alpaca, vicuña, puma and so on).

MONUMENT TO BÉCQUER

14

An emotional and secret garden

Parque de María Luisa
Glorieta de Bécquer

If each park keeps a secret, then María Luisa's secret is to be found on the Glorieta de Bécquer. This secluded roundabout features a living monument, in constant flux, paying tribute to the life and work of Romantic writer Gustavo Adolfo Bécquer, a poet, literary columnist and playwright who was born in Seville in 1836 and died in Madrid at the age of 36.

To feel the emotional intensity of this verdant spot you have to walk around the monument in a complete circle, following the paths of passion in the sculptures and soaking up the light as it filters through the fine cypress tree leaves. And thereby feel *the invisible atoms of the air …* The majestic tree, which is the heart of the monument, was planted in the mid-19th century in what was then the private garden of the Duke and Duchess of Montpensier. It was here that French gardener André Lecolant embarked on a landscaping project based on the imitation of wild nature. The bald cypress that stands here dates from that period, a deciduous conifer originating from the swampy regions of the Mississippi river basin and therefore quite at home in close proximity to the Guadalquivir. It currently measures some 40 metres tall and 3 metres across, and could live at least 300 years.

In 1893 the widowed infanta María Luisa Fernanda gifted her garden to the city of Seville. The town hall named it after her, and subsequently commissioned French landscape gardener Forestier to carry out reforms. Years later María Luisa's park was chosen to act as host venue for the Ibero-American Expo held in 1929.

December 1911 (before Forestier's reform but once the park had been opened to the public) saw the inauguration of the monument to the Romantic poet, thanks to the initiative of the Álvarez Quintero brothers, Seville playwrights who donated the rights to their work *La Rima Eterna* (*The Eternal Rhyme*) to help fund the project. Sculptor Lorenzo Coullaut Valera designed a circular bench that girdles the tree and which has to be regularly widened to cater for the ever-growing cypress. Next to the half-length statue of Bécquer, three female figures carved in Italian white marble represent the poet's Rhyme number X, *El amor que pasa* (*Love that Passes By*) in its three stages, present, past and future. Completing the ensemble are two bronze statues: a winged cupid searching for passion with his bow and an injured one lying on the ground with his wings broken.

ENIGMA MACHINE

15

The Nazis' secret messages

Museo Histórico Militar
Plaza de España (Puerta de Aragón)
954 93 82 83
Monday–Friday 9.30am–2pm, Saturday 10am–2pm
Admission free

One of the most unusual features housed at the Museo Histórico Militar (Museum of Military History), and unknown to the vast majority of Seville locals, is a perfectly preserved example of the Enigma cipher machine used by Nazi Germany. Although Enigma gave the Third Reich a decisive advantage during the early stages of the Second World War, Hitler had already road-tested it in Spain during the military conflict following Franco's 1936 coup d'état.

With the Nationalist offensive at a standstill on the Madrid front, the rebels asked Germany to sell them 10 Enigma machines, which were used by Francoist representatives in Berlin and Rome and by top-ranking military commanders, including those leading the Southern Army. The intention was to avoid the Republican government forces from deciphering their telegraph messages from one front to another, as both sides were using the same communications techniques.

This particular Enigma machine is identified as code number A1234, weighs some 11.5 kg and is similar to a typewriter, but without the carriage or roller for the paper. It has three rows of keys with the 26 letters of the alphabet and the numbers 0 to 9, a panel with the same letters that light up, and some little windows in which either letters or numbers appear. Thanks to its mechanism, it could produce millions of combinations of letters and numbers, which made it impossible for receivers to decipher its messages other than by using another Enigma machine.

Alan Turing, the Briton who broke the Enigma code

Breaking the Enigma code called for the emergence of the figure of Alan Turing, a British mathematician, philosopher and cryptographer. As part of project codename 'Ultra', he was enlisted by the British Secret Service to work at Bletchley Park, a Victorian mansion that concealed a secret military base, in collaboration with a large number of expert cryptographers, mostly women. It was thus that, thanks to Turing's work breaking the German code in the final years of the Second World War, the Allies were able to anticipate Nazi military movements.

In addition to his crucial role in bringing the war to an end, Turing's research was a precursor to the subsequent development of information technology and cybernetics. He carried out the first design for an automatic computer, and is considered the father of artificial intelligence. However, in 1952 none of that would save him from being convicted as a homosexual and sentenced to chemical castration and subsequently being fired from his job. Two years later he took his own life by eating a cyanide-laced apple.

CERAMIC MAPS OF SEVILLE IN PLAZA DE ESPAÑA

16

An early 20th-century tourist guide

Plaza de España
Parque de María Luisa
Daily 8am–10pm

One of Seville's iconic hotspots par excellence, Plaza de España, conceals a good number of secrets and oddities that most visitors fail to spot.

The maps made from ceramic tiles for the 1929 Ibero-American Expo are one such curiosity. They were arranged on the ground towards the front of the square where there are also 48 ceramic murals, each referring to one historical fact from its respective Spanish province.

At the beginning of the first series of arches, on the ground behind the north tower, there is a colourful tile map of the city's monuments, marking the location of the main attractions and serving as an early 20th-century tourist guide. The map was originally created in the factory of Pedro Navia, using the *cuerda seca* (dry cord) technique, and then rearranged by the Plaza de España workshop school in 2004. The same map may be found at the end of the square in front of the south tower.

Just before the Puerta de Aragón entrance there is a map depicting agricultural Seville, and then the strangest one of all, a ceramic map of

Roman Seville featuring the vestiges of that period distributed across the entire province. Finally, on either side of the Puerta de Navarra entrance are maps dedicated to the city's agricultural and cattle-breeding aspects.

Ammonite fossils

On the stone balustrade of the bridge of the Kingdom of Aragon are large ammonite fossils dating back some 250 million years.

Spain embraces the Ibero-American countries

Designed by architect Aníbal González, Plaza de España was conceived of as one of the 1929 Expo's central attractions. With its semi-elliptical shape and 200-metre diameter, it represents Spain embracing the Ibero-American countries, pointing to the Guadalquivir as the natural channel of communications with the Latin American continent.

Treasure of European film culture

The square was designated a Treasure of European Film Culture, given that the space has been used as a film location on numerous occasions, for movies including *Lawrence of Arabia* and *Star Wars*.

ARGENTINIAN PAVILION FROM THE 1929 EXPO

Scenes from the Pampas and pre-Hispanic figures

Conservatorio Profesional de Danza Antonio Ruiz Soler
Paseo de las Delicias
Monday–Friday 4pm–8pm
Visits by prior appointment: danzasevillaconservatorio@gmail.com
conservatoriodanzasevilla.com

O ne of the most impressive pavilions to be erected for the 1929 Ibero-American Expo was the Argentinian one. Nowadays, this

historic building remains a hidden secret for most Seville locals, other than students and teaching staff at the Professional Dance Conservatory which has had its headquarters here since 1994.

Argentinian architect Martín San Noel was the man behind its neo-colonial design, including elements from pre-Hispanic cultures alongside Baroque and Renaissance ones, as seen on the main façade.

The pavilion is made up of various buildings interconnected by a central patio. In the area to the right is a great hall covered by an octagonal dome decorated with colourful tile ensembles featuring pre-Hispanic figures designed by the great Seville painter Gustavo Bacarisas. He also made a number of paintings that once decorated the upper area, now on display in this very hall. This was the location of the industrial exhibition showing off the country's advances.

The left wing houses a theatre seating over 200 people, used for conference addresses and film projections.

Climbing the monumental stairway, you're confronted with a series of landscapes and Argentinian genre scenes, also designed by Bacarisas and produced in the Montalván ceramics factory in Triana. Argentinian artists Alfredo Guido, Rodolfo Franco and Alfredo Gramajo also contributed to the overall decoration.

On the upper floor there is a magnificent library, now used as a dance studio. This is one of the oddest parts of the building, where the eye is drawn to the noble woods of the coffered ceiling, carved balconies and huge bookshelves. Another interesting feature is the spectacular vantage point in the main tower of the pavilion, with a room also boasting a luxurious coffered wood ceiling from which visitors can marvel at a fully panoramic view of both river and city.

NEARBY
Guatemalan Pavilion
Paseo de las Delicias (no number)

Just along from the Argentinian one, the Guatemalan installation was among the most modest at the 1929 Expo, though that doesn't mean the

pavilion is of no interest. Today used as an annex of the Dance Conservatory, the building's most prominent feature is on the outside, which is covered by blue and white tiles. These are the work of Ramos Rejano, with figures from Mayan culture and two spectacular images of the quetzal bird.

CERVANTES IN THE ROUND

Knight of the Sad Countenance

Plaza de América
Parque de María Luisa

Surrounding an impressive araucaria (monkey puzzle) tree in the gardens of Plaza de América, just opposite the Pabellón Real, you might stumble onto one of the Parque María Luisa's most secretively hidden gems: four benches covered with tiles depicting episodes from Miguel de Cervantes' masterpiece, *Don Quixote de la Mancha*.

To follow the famous knight's adventures, you have to follow the tiles from left to right and top to bottom. A comic strip more than a hundred years old where none of the images has any text other than the last tile, featuring the novel's final epitaph: 'it was his great good fortune to live a madman and die sane'.

This space is completed by two ceramic shelves, which originally housed the works of Cervantes to be read in the shade of the trees. At the ends of each of these bookshelves there were once clay busts depicting Don Quixote and Sancho Panza, now housed in the Moroccan Pavilion from the 1929 Expo (see p. 260). Their decoration includes a range of illustrations of both Cervantes and his literary creation, and there are

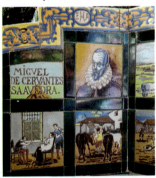

shelves with plaques marking significant dates in the life of the author, starting with his birth in Alcalá de Henares in 1547.

This little octagonal plaza was designed by local architect Aníbal González in 1913, for the 1929 Ibero-American Expo. Manufactured using the *cuerda seca* (dry cord) technique in Ramos Rejano's Triana workshops, the tiles were the work of ceramic painter Pedro Borrego.

Cervantes in Seville

There's no better way of finding out about the life and customs of 16th-century 'Sevillanos' than to leaf through some of Cervantes' exemplary novels dedicated to the city, such as *Rinconete and Cortadillo* and *The Spanish English Lady*. At the end of that century he was employed as the royal supplies commissioner in Andalusia, in charge of stocks of oil and wheat for Philip II's Invincible Armada. His endeavours would set him at odds with the Church and he was excommunicated twice. Later, in 1597, he was incarcerated in the Royal Prison on Seville's Calle Sierpes, where he underwent a crash course in picaresque hand-to-mouth living, as reflected in his writing. In 1916, to mark the third centenary of Cervantes' death, the city paid tribute to him by installing 20 ceramic plaques (one is now lost) in the places throughout Seville mentioned in his works.

MEXICAN PAVILION FROM THE 1929 EXPO

A building conceived of as a Mayan-Toltec temple

Universidad de Sevilla
Corner of Paseo de las Delicias and Avenida de Eritaña
Monday–Friday 9.30am–1.30pm

On Paseo de las Delicias, just around the corner from María Luisa park, stands the Mexican Pavilion from the 1929 Ibero-American Expo. As the pavilion is currently being used as Seville University office space, you can visit the areas open to the public in this iconic and yet little-known building.

Yucatán-born architect Manuel María Amábilis came up with the concept for the 1929 Expo as a temple, drawing on the iconography of Mayan and Toltec culture. With a floorplan in the shape of a double X (representing the merging of Aztec and Spanish cultures in Mexico), it was the only pavilion built in a neo-indigenous style.

The main entrance is guarded by two Quetzalcóatl serpents, the symbol of the god of life and fertility. Known as the *feathered serpent*, this figure also features in the beautiful polychrome fountain on the rear façade. The upper section is crowned by a tympanum with reliefs depicting five figures joined by garlands and guarded by two reclining human figures. These are Chac-Mool, exact replicas of those found in the Mayan city of Chichén Itzá. According to some theories, this sort of statue served as an altar where offerings were left for the god of rain, as well as being a sacrificial stone.

All that's left of the building's interesting glasswork is one pane from the skylight over the central foyer, which features the Mexican coat of arms with an eagle holding a serpent in its beak and perched on a prickly pear tree, seen coming out of a lagoon (all the rest was lost during the many uses the building has been put to).

Along the stairway two niches have survived, with statues dedicated to an Aztec warrior and a Spanish conquistador. Towards the top of the stairs there were once mural paintings in which Diego Rivera participated. Sadly, these have since disappeared.

NEARBY

Cuban Pavilion

Agencia Andaluza de Cooperación Internacional para el Desarrollo
Avenida de la Palmera, 24
Monday–Friday 9am–2pm

The Cuban Pavilion, which was also built for the 1929 Expo, is an interesting example of colonial architecture influenced by models from Andalusia and the Canary Islands. The spectacular portico is made from Jaimanita stone, a mineral originating from coral and brought from the island. Inside is a stunning carved mahogany stairway with a magnificent sculpted mascaron (grotesque mask) crowning a lamp, along with the huge range of noble Caribbean timber used in the construction of the pavilion, including mahogany, sabicu, yabá, sapodilla and fiddle wood.

COLOMBIAN PAVILION FROM THE 1929 EXPO

Sacred nature in pre-Columbian cultures

Colombian Consulate
Paseo de las Delicias
csevilla@cancilleria.gov.co
Admission free by prior appointment

The Colombian Pavilion from the 1929 Ibero-American Expo is reminiscent of Latin American Baroque architecture, with some astonishing decoration that draws inspiration from pre-Columbian

indigenous cultures, reinterpreted through art deco forms by Colombian sculptor Rómulo Rozo. The building currently houses the Colombian Consulate, but is open to the public by prior appointment.

The main façade features the myth of Bochica, the Sun god and creator of the arts and civilisation, depicted in the celestial sphere towards the top. The myth of the origin of humankind is represented towards the bottom of the pavilion. The two worlds are separated by a ceramic frieze symbolising the ritual procession and sacrifice of Guesa, a child raised in the Sun temple who was led by a procession of masked priests to the pillar of Bochica, to which he was tied and then shot at with arrows, his heart finally being offered to the Sun god.

Two coiled serpents guard the entrance, as in the temple of Bachué, the mother-goddess of the Chibcha people, reflecting the myth of the snake-woman. The main doorway is flanked by the figures of two warrior goddesses dressed sumptuously and covered in necklaces, bracelets and colourful feathers.

The mouldings around the doors represent the Earth through maize and flowers, and the Air through tongues of fire.

The magnificent iron gateway is a reference to the myth of the Muisca culture regarding the journey made by souls to the centre of the Earth, traversing rivers and crossing ravines in rafts made from spiders' webs. In the middle of the gate there is a sacred frog on top of a warrior's weapons, and an underground river represented by fretwork depicting fish and frogs, which also feature on the balconies of the towers. In the culture's mythological symbolism, an extended frog stood for happiness, bountiful harvests and domestic plenty, being considered above all as a sacred animal with a protective function.

The foyer is dominated by two large-scale mosaics portraying Colombia's relationship with the world and with the Iberian Peninsula, leading on to a large patio with a gallery reminiscent of colonial houses, including the coats of arms of Quimbaya warriors as well as four enormous dragonflies in the corners, representing bad luck, love, rain and the harvest.

MOROCCAN PAVILION FROM THE 1929 EXPO

An interesting selection of Moroccan architecture and craftsmanship

Avenida de Molíní, 4
Monday–Friday 9am–2pm

A large building just a stone's throw from the portside installations makes you wonder whether this is Seville or some Moroccan city. The former Moroccan Pavilion, built for the 1929 Ibero-American Expo, has served as the headquarters of the City's Parks and Gardens Services since 1957. Although the outside gives the impression of a mosque with whitewashed walls and dome, while its square tower is reminiscent of a minaret, inside visitors are immersed in an exhibition space conceived of as a *riad*, a luxurious and exotic residence.

Passing through the entranceway presided over by a triple horseshoe arch, you find yourself in a large central patio covered by a glass skylight roof with four carved wooden balconies supported by octagonal pillars and, in the middle, a white marble fountain with a mosaic basin.

The magnificent decorative features including plasterwork, coffered ceilings, ceramics, carved wooden doors and iron grilles were carried out by the School of Indigenous Arts in Tetuán. The art school director, José Gutiérrez Lescura, also designed the pavilion, assisted in the decorative aspects by renowned painter Mariano Bertuchi.

Access to the adjoining rooms is through five large solid wooden doors, which have been carved and polychromed with Islamic-style tracery. At the back of the pavilion is the main room, known as the Salón Moro (Moor's Room), which along with all the rest of the spaces represents the nature, culture and history of what at that time was the Spanish Protectorate of Morocco.

A little souk was built around the building, where numerous artisans would give live demonstrations of their trades, including gold and silverwork, leather, ceramics, embroidery, tapestry and so on.

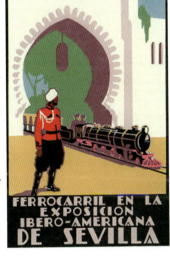

The pavilion was complemented by what was then known as the Barrio Moro (Moor's Quarter). This complex, just across the road, was made up of shops, little coffee houses and other venues where you could watch traditional shows, and even included a mosque and a *hammam* (Arab baths). The miniature train that toured the Expo enclosure also had one of its six stops here (see p. 60).

Sadly, neither of these two buildings has survived to the present day.

FAIRBAIRN CRANE

A souvenir from the port of Seville

Calle Alfonso XIII

At the southern headwaters of Las Delicias dock, just next to Naval Command headquarters, you'll find the Fairbairn Crane, the oldest port crane (*grúa*) in Seville.

With its curved shape and sea-blue colour the crane looks rather out of place where it stands, some distance from the river bank. The Seville port authorities purchased it from Manchester's Fairbairn company in 1874, with the intention of installing it on the Sal (Salt) docks just along from Isabel II or, as it's more commonly known, Triana bridge.

Port activity gradually shifted south of the river to the Nueva York docks, to where our crane was also moved in 1905. It would stay there

for over a century, on the docks from which the transatlantic passenger liners set sail for the United States, until taken to its present resting place.

Costing more than 100,000 pesetas at the time, the port authorities' construction board purchased it to meet the needs of the railway company, the city's shipowners and the owners of a foundry.

The crane is named after the man who designed it, Sir William Fairbairn, who in 1850 came up with the notion of the curved 11-metre arm and the use of a steam boiler, attaining a lifting strength of up to 40 tonnes as opposed to the 3 tonnes achieved by conventional cranes. This meant that in its day it was considered the most advanced crane in Spain.

Apart from the Seville Fairbairn (the only one in Spain) only a handful of cranes of this model have survived out of all those mass-installed during the port expansions of the late 19th century. These are currently in Bristol and Dover (United Kingdom) and Helsingor (Denmark).

NEARBY
Naval Pavilion ⑧
Comandancia Naval de Sevilla Avenida Guadalhorce (no number)
Avenida de Molini, 6

Dedicated to the Spanish navy during the 1929 Ibero-American Expo, this Regionalist-style pavilion was the work of architect Vicente Traver. Of particular note is the clock tower including neo-Baroque details, and a glazed ceramic border with the coats of arms of 20 prominent naval officers from the history of the Spanish fleets. Famous surnames include Pinzón (who accompanied Columbus), Ulloa and Pardo de Figueroa. The building has been used as the headquarters of Naval Command since 1933.

Capitanía Marítima ⑨
Avenida Guadalhorce (no number)

Located next to Las Delicias bridge, this building was also designed by Traver for the 1929 Ibero-American Expo. Known as the 'Pavilion for Customs and Customs Officer Services', it was used as a train station for Expo visitors (see p. 60). The pavilion was renovated in 2008 to house the city Harbourmaster's office.

PORT INFORMATION CENTRE'S REPLICA OF THE 'INGENIO'

Used in the construction of the cathedral

Autoridad Portuaria de Sevilla
Avenida de las Razas, 24
954 24 73 37
portal.apsevilla.com
museo@apsevilla.com
Monday–Friday 8am–2pm
Admission free on booking a guided tour

A series of warehouses was built in the port area for the 1929 Ibero-American Expo. These have bare brick walls featuring interesting ceramic ornamentation and fruit motifs. Since 1999, warehouses 4–5 have housed a curious museum that explains the role of Seville's port over the centuries.

The fascinating tour takes visitors from the founding of the port when the Phoenicians installed the first anchorage, followed by the Romans who established a major river port in Hispalis, through the construction of the Ataranzas (medieval shipyards promoted by Alfonso X) to the port's key role in the discovery of the Americas, concluding with its future and present, currently consisting of 38 hectares of various docks and a 5 km berthing line.

The area with the old cranes is of particular interest, including a large-scale replica of the 'Ingenio' (Machine), the original crane installed next to the Torre del Oro in the early 15th century, as may be observed from a number of historical engravings. It was used to unload the huge stone blocks for the construction of the cathedral, and continued to operate until the 17th century. Also of note is the old 1842 crane cast in the prominent El Pedroso foundry in Seville's northern 'sierra' mountain range.

All of these elements point to the maritime side of the city, something also reminiscent of the tides that rise up the Guadalquivir every day, only to subside on reaching its port.

From the Guadalquivir estuary on the Atlantic coast in Sanlúcar de Barrameda (Cádiz) you have to sail some 90 km upstream, a trip taking about five hours, before passing the great floodgates and reaching the port of Seville.

MUSEO DE HISTORIA DE LA FARMACIA

Tour of a little-known 19th-century apothecary

Facultad de Farmacia. Universidad de Sevilla
Calle Profesor García González, 2. Basement
954 55 67 29
antonioramos@us.es
institucional.us.es/museohistfarm
Tours by prior appointment

If you book in advance, you can join a tour of the little-known Museum of the History of Pharmacy in the basement of Seville's Pharmacy Faculty. Passing through its doors, you suddenly enter a late 19th- or early 20th-century chemist's emporium and embark on an interesting and surprising tour of the ancient art of healing.

The great office desk from the former Gallego pharmacy, alongside the antique cash register, set the tone of the space. It was from here that the public was provided with medication. Just behind the desk, a door leads to the office and the back room where the chemist mixed his drugs.

On display are all sorts of period instruments: mortars and scales, pill boxes, moulds for rectal or vaginal suppositories, along with other tools for making master recipes and medications.

With the advance of science, laboratories started to play an increasingly important role, giving rise to items such as microscopes, areometers, centrifuges, burners and so on.

The shelves are heaving with an incredible collection of pharmaceutical products: pills, syrups, elixirs, balms ... including a rare collection of homeopathic products from the mid-19th century. They demonstrate the evolution from the most artisan of production processes to the emerging industry that would come into conflict with traditional pharmaceutics and hold out for some years, continuing to prepare medications for the public.

Remounting the stairs, the hallway to the right houses the shelves from two of Seville's traditional pharmacies.

The great mahogany shelves, with part of their original collection of jars, were once on display in Murillo's pharmacy, founded in Plaza del Salvador in 1897 by Francisco Murillo Hernández (see p. 210). Opposite them are shelves from the chemist's that used to be located on Calle Feria, founded by Eloy Burgos Nevado in 1913.

TOWER OF THE CÓRDOBA PAVILION

All that remains of the Córdoba Pavilion from the 1929 Expo

Avenida de Reina Mercedes, 4

Seville University students who frequent Avenida de Reina Mercedes, where most of the technical and science faculties are located, will

be more than well-acquainted with a slender tower standing some 15 metres tall. But few will know the origins of this watchtower that keeps vigilant guard over the campus gardens, with no apparent connection to the surrounding buildings.

The tower is all that's left of the Córdoba Pavilion from Seville's 1929 Ibero-American Expo. Its lower section was made up of a vaulted space, whose shape can be discerned if one turns the construction upside down, linking up with the great reception hall based on the Córdoba Mezquita's forest of caliphate-era pillars.

The tower itself was inspired by that of Córdoba's church of San Nicolás de la Villa, the oldest and perhaps most beautiful in the city. Construction began during the reign of the Catholic Monarchs in 1494 and was completed two years later. On the site of the old minaret of an Islamic mosque, it consists of two sections, the first being four-sided and the second octagonal, crowned by a small belfry added in the 18th century.

The pavilion was designed by the Córdoba municipal architect Carlos Sáenz de Santamaría, and was inaugurated just a few months before the end of the Exposition.

During the Expo, the great Córdoban painter Julio Romero de Torres exhibited a wide selection of his works, including what would be his last and best-known painting, *La Chiquita Piconera* (*Young Girl with Coal Brazier*). On 10 May 1930, soon after the pavilion first opened its doors, the artist died and his family decided not to sell the paintings he had put on display, instead donating them to Córdoba City Council, and thereby sowing the seeds for what would become the Julio Romero de Torres Museum. Currently, and as a reminder of this story, the tower stands as the sole surviving part of the Córdoba Pavilion.

NEARBY
Seville Pavilion from the 1929 Expo
Casino de la Exposición – Glorieta San Diego
casinodelaexposicion.org

Of the pavilions representing the Andalusian provinces, Seville's is the only one still standing. It was made up of the Expo Casino and the Lope de Vega Theatre, designed in a neo-Baroque style by architect Vicente Traver.

Cartuja Island and San Jerónimo

OMBÚ TREE IN LA CARTUJA

The first tree from the Americas to be planted in Seville

Cartuja de Santa María de Las Cuevas
Avenida Américo Vespucio, 2

Opposite the front of Santa María de las Cuevas monastery on the Isla de la Cartuja there is a huge and ancient ombú tree that could be over four hundred years old. As it doesn't have growth rings like some trees do, it's difficult to determine its age, but this ombú may have been the first tree from the Americas to be planted in Seville.

According to legend, it was planted after Ferdinand Columbus, the second son of Christopher, returned from his trip to the Americas, though neither father nor son were ever in what is now Argentina and Uruguay, from where the tree originates.

In 1502, the 13-year-old Ferdinand accompanied his father on his fourth and final expedition to the Americas, and in 1509, three years after the death of Christopher, he travelled with his brother Diego to take up governorship of Hispaniola (now the Dominican Republic and Haiti). Before that trip, the two brothers buried their father in the chapel of Santa Ana in Santa María de las Cuevas monastery, having transported his remains from Valladolid.

Next to the ombú, a statue of Columbus donated in the 19th century by the widow of the Marquis of Pickman (see p. 277) commemorates this fact and his numerous stays here.

Ombú is a Guaraní word meaning 'shade', something much sought after on the open plains of the tree's native Argentina and Uruguay. For some, the ombú (scientific name *Phytolacca dioica*) is more a bush than a tree – a huge bush certainly, made up of light woody and fleshy boughs that enable it to store large quantities of water, and with a toxic sap that repels insects.

Ferdinand Columbus, Renaissance man

Ferdinand Columbus (1488–1539) represents the multifaceted personality of the Renaissance man. His interest in exploration and cosmography were complemented by his two genuine passions as a bibliophile and botanist. Throughout his life he travelled to Italy, France, Switzerland, Belgium, Germany and more, building up one of Europe's foremost book collections.

On his death he left it to Seville cathedral (where he's buried), making up what is now the Biblioteca Colombina (see p. 142). In his palace, which once stood near the Puerta Real, he created Seville's first botanical garden, and the biggest one in Europe, acclimatising a great number of plants brought back from the Americas.

TOMB OF DIEGO GÓMEZ DE RIBERA

A fatal mouth injury

Sala Capitular
Monasterio de la Cartuja
Centro Andaluz de Arte Contemporáneo
Avenida Américo Vespucio, 2
caac.es
Tuesday–Saturday 11am–9pm, Sunday & public holidays 11am–3.30pm

In the Sala Capitular (Chapter Hall) of the Carthusian monastery of Santa María de la Cuevas there is a Gothic-style burial chapel dedicated to the Ribera family. On the left as you go in your eye is drawn to the tomb of Diego Gómez de Ribera, the second 'Adelantado Mayor' of Andalusia, a sort of captain-general appointed by the king in the border conflicts with the Kingdom of Granada.

Judging by his posture, you'd think the knight was snoring peacefully, almost with his back to his wife, Beatriz Portocarrero, daughter of the lord of Moguer. Dressed in armour and helmet, he holds his sword in his right hand, with his left leg crossing over his right, protecting the weapon as if someone was trying to wrest it from him. But, if you look closely, the forced grimace in his mouth is an indication of the wound that led to the violent death highlighted by the sculptor.

We know that Diego Gómez de Ribera was the son of Per Afán de Ribera, known as 'The Elder', the first Adelantado Mayor of Andalusia, and Aldonza de Ayala, his second wife, but neither his date or place of birth are known. What is known is the date of his death in 1434, in the attack on the fortress of Álora in Malaga. Having conquered Iznájar in the Kingdom of Granada and a large number of other fortresses, and having been victorious in many battles with the Moors, Gómez de Ribera laid siege to the town of Álora and was shot in the mouth by a crossbow just as he was raising his bevor (armour to protect the neck) to parley. And that is the wound depicted here. The *Romance de Álora*, a famous piece from the old frontier poetry repertory, gives a dramatic and almost journalistic account of his death. It records that while the Moors were fleeing the fortress, voices could be heard from the castle battlements asking for a ceasefire and offering to hand over the fortress. When the Christian captain lifted his visor to see who was surrendering, a hidden Moor shot him in the face with a crossbow bolt. In the poem two individuals Gómez de Ribera had raised from infants, Pablo and Jacobillo, appear and rescue their mortally wounded lord, who tells them his last will and testament with his dying breath.

CHIMNEYS OF LA CARTUJA

One of the few, and most beautiful, examples of the city's industrial heritage

Centro Andaluz de Arte Contemporáneo
Cartuja de Santa María de Las Cuevas, Avenida Américo Vespucio, 2
caac.es
Tuesday–Saturday 11am–9pm, Sunday & public holidays 11am–3.30pm

A t the back of the old monastery of La Cartuja (15th century), which now serves as the Centro Andaluz de Arte Contemporáneo (Andalusian Centre for Contemporary Art), three enormous and perfectly preserved pottery bottle ovens are discreetly tucked away. Not easy to locate, you need to cross the patio where the centre's café is and walk round the building to the right, through the gardens and orange

groves, also passing the little-known drying ovens on the way. Oddly enough, the very existence of these chimney ovens is a mystery to most Seville locals, despite being one of the few (and most beautiful) examples of the city's industrial heritage: the former Pickman-La Cartuja Ceramics Factory. The great brick chimney nicknamed 'El Gran Capitán' is a more popular feature, due to its towering 30-metre height and location in the cloisters of the old monastery, alongside two other bottle ovens. Of no less interest are the Horno del Cuarzo (Quartz Oven) and Horno de Oro (Gold Oven), despite barely meriting a second glance in the patio of the Instituto Andaluz de Patrimonio Histórico (Andalusian Institute for Historical Heritage) as you go in through the river (Río) entrance, from where you can make out the chimney bearing the same name.

Bottle ovens

These chimneys, which get their name from their bottle-like shape, were a genuine feat of innovation in the 19th-century English ceramics industry. The heat produced in the lower of the two chambers through the combustion of coal passes through the upper chamber via a series of holes, firing the pieces of pottery and hardening the glaze.

Charles Pickman's Factory

The ceramics factory in La Cartuja was founded by English entrepreneur Charles Pickman, who purchased the Santa María de la Cuevas monastery in 1839, adapting it to the manufacture of pottery and porcelain. Its output achieved international renown, including a wide range of items from tiles and firebricks to bathroom fittings, but mostly artistic ceramics and household earthenware. Dinner services featuring drawings of local Seville landscapes were La Cartuja's most iconic product, and have continued to be manufactured throughout its history. By the late 19th century the factory employed as many as 1,200 workers and was a leader in Spain, until industrial activity was shut down here in 1981, moving to the town of Salteras where it's still up and running today. The monastery was the Royal Pavilion at the 1992 Universal Exposition.

PICKMAN PAVILION

The secret buildings of La Cartuja's Huerta Grande

Centro Andaluz de Arte Contemporáneo
Cartuja de Santa María de Las Cuevas
Avenida Américo Vespucio, 2
Access to Huerta Grande through café patio
Tuesday–Saturday 11am–9pm, Sunday & public holidays 11am–3.30pm

Oner of the most secluded and little-known green spaces in the city, La Cartuja's Huerta Grande (Great Orchard) is an ethnological and landscaping relic surrounding the old Carthusian monastery, accessed by crossing a patio known as 'Padre Nuestro' (Our Father). Hidden among fruit and cypress trees, and tucked away behind the monastery that was converted into a ceramics factory in 1841 (see p. 276), is an unexpected building known as the Pickman Pavilion.

Built on the site of a 16th-century former chapel dedicated to the patron saints of Seville, Justa and Rufina, it was commissioned by factory-owner Charles Pickford. The building, designed by Juan Lizasoáin in an Orientalist style reminiscent of 19th-century British pleasure garden pavilions, is open on all four sides of the ground floor, and features a little tower with a lookout. The exotic mystery of the place is heightened thanks to a permanent installation by artist Olaf Nicolai, entitled *Black Pearls Curtain*, designed in 2004 for Seville's 1st Biennale of Contemporary Art.

From here you can enjoy the fantastic panoramic view of the enormous orchard with more than three thousand orange, lemon and other fruit trees planted by Carthusian monks. Since it was founded in the 15th century, La Cartuja has steadily grown, finally becoming a self-sufficient little settlement with various hectares given over to its orchards and gardens, including fruit trees, medicinal herbs for the pharmacy and a complex irrigation system inherited from Andalusian farming practices, all surrounded by walls for safety and protection from flooding.

NEARBY
Chapel of Santa Ana

Among the system of old orchards there is another beautiful pleasure garden pavilion, the fruit of the neo-Gothic renovation of a former chapel dedicated to St Anne in the 16th century. This shrine, decorated with interesting alfresco paintings, was the site of a number of meetings between St Teresa of Ávila and the prior of the monastery, her protector in Seville, as she was denied access to the enclosed monastery.

The building looks over an irrigation reservoir that supplied water along old channels and through sluices, brought up from the nearby river by a pair of waterwheels, the remains of which survive to this day.

MOROCCAN PAVILION FROM EXPO '92

A hidden archaeological gem

Fundación Tres Culturas del Mediterráneo
Calle Max Planck, 2
tresculturas.org
Guided tours by prior appointment, Tuesday 11am–noon

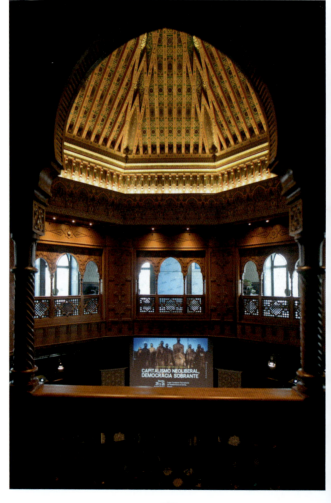

The pavilion that represented Morocco at Expo '92 is a hidden gem whose image as a lavish Arabian palace has been well preserved thanks to its function as headquarters for the Three Cultures of the Mediterranean Foundation.

Designed by French architect Michel Pinseau, who was also responsible for the Hassan II mosque in Casablanca (the second largest in the world), its façades present a rich array of traditional Arab-Islamic styles including latticework, fountains and tiled walls.

Furthermore, its beautifully decorated interior features a multitude of artisan building techniques (which required more than 600 craftsmen to be brought over from Morocco): carved and coloured woods, plasterwork, ceramic murals and wall surfaces, for which such unexpected ingredients as sand, black soap and egg were used. The basement level (the pavilion's hidden oasis) and the central patio, with its series of carved wooden balconies and spectacular moving dome with polychrome coffered ceiling, are of particular interest.

Eight-pointed star

The pavilion's floorplan is shaped like an eight-pointed star, a motif to be found all over the building in mirrors, fountains, lamps, doors, handles, lattices and so on. This symbol, which goes by the name *Rub el Hizb* (fourth part), is used in the Koran to mark the end of chapters, and was considered a representation of paradise, which was thought to be surrounded by eight mountains.

HUNGARIAN PAVILION FROM EXPO '92

Seven towers that look like a rural Hungarian church

Calle Marie Curie

Thanks to its designation as an Asset of Cultural Interest on the grounds of its major archaeological value, the spectacular Hungarian Pavilion from the Universal Exposition of 1992 managed

to avoid being demolished, though not the state of neglect in which it now languishes.

The wood and slate building, designed by architect Imre Makovecz, one of the most important proponents of so-called organic architecture, was one of the most highly rated pavilions among Expo visitors, even if now consigned to oblivion.

It represents a rural Hungarian church crowned by seven towers on which bronze bells were installed to commemorate the Hungarian victory over the Ottoman empire at the battle of Belgrade in 1456.

The entire roof is covered by grey tiles, giving the impression of the inverted hull of a ship, while the entrances are presided over by great mascarons made from a reddish wood.

NEARBY
Finnish Pavilion from Expo '92

Fundación para la Investigación y Difusión de la Arquitectura, Sevilla (FIDAS)
Calle Marie Curie, 3
Isla de la Cartuja
Monday–Friday 8am–3pm

Although Finland's installation was designed to be temporary, its enormous aesthetic attraction has transformed it into the first from that country to be preserved after a World's Fair. The pavilion is made up of two opposing and complementary buildings: Kone (machine), made from cold steel, symbolising industry and technology; and Koli (keel), made from wood, in reference to nature and tradition. There is a narrow gap between the two, representing Hell's Hole, a metaphor for the symbolic cleft in Helvetinjärvi National Park.

Mexican Pavilion from Expo '92

Calle Tomás Alba Edison, 6

In spite of its current state of neglect, the Mexican Pavilion was one of the buildings with the most unusual and significant attractive features from Expo '92. Under two enormous 18-metre Xs, the letter representing the name of the country as well as referring back to the pavilion of 1929 (see p. 256), there is an exact replica of a 3-metre Olmec head. In front of the building, a large-scale coloured mosaic alludes to *God's Eye*, a ritual and magical artefact for the Huichol and Tepehuán indigenous peoples, also known as *Tsikuri*, meaning 'to be able to see and understand unknown things'. It's something of a surprise to find a giant cactus next to the pavilion. This 'saguaro' (*Carnegiea gigantea*) comes from the deserts of the Valley of the Giants in Mexicali, Baja California, stands some 14 metres tall, weighs 18 tonnes, and is estimated to be hundreds of years old.

ALAMILLO PARK MONUMENT TO 'SIR'

A lesson on nature

Parque del Alamillo
Calle Anular
parquedelalamillo.org
November–March 7am–8pm
April, May & October 7am–10pm
June & September 7am–midnight
July & August 7am–2am

Alamillo park lies just north of the Isla de la Cartuja municipal city limits. If you go through the main entrance and walk 300 metres along Calle Anular, in the middle of the lawn to your left you'll spot a curious sculptural tribute to the teaching profession. The bronze monument depicts a classroom scene from the 1930s with two period desks, at one of which a girl is sitting listening to the lesson being given by a male teacher approaching retirement age.

The scene is completed by an implied blackboard which leaves the whole natural backdrop of this green space on view.

Inaugurated in 2003, *El homenaje al maestro* (Tribute to the Teacher) was the work of Ignacio Sancho Caparrini, a sculptor from Zaragoza who had settled in Seville.

Located between the old and new courses of the Guadalquivir, Alamillo park is the fruit of a land regeneration project for Seville's 1992 Universal Exposition. It currently measures some 85 hectares, and there are plans to expand it to 120 hectares, which would make it one of the biggest urban parks in Spain. The most interesting thing about this popular space is its landscape design, which features local vegetation (holm oaks, pines, cork trees, wild olives), transforming it into an excellent example of Mediterranean forest and a great place for birdwatching.

NEARBY
Alamillo miniature railway ⑩
Next to the north entrance
Sunday 11am –2pm

Installed in 2002, the park's miniature railway is managed by the Seville Association of Friends of the Railway. Along its 250-metre circuit and 150 metres of secondary tracks run model trains of all sorts on which visitors can take a sit-down ride. It also features a little main station and another secondary one, a train depot, a workshop with a pit and a railway turntable, along with two main trains, others with auxiliary functions, and various sets of carriages.

COLUMBUS' EGG SCULPTURE

The biggest bronze sculpture in Spain

Parque de San Jerónimo

Weighing some 476 tonnes, standing 42 metres tall and supported by a base 32 metres across, Columbus' Egg in San Jerónimo park is the biggest sculpture in Spain.

It portrays Christopher Columbus holding a nautical chart featuring the three caravels with which he discovered America, all framed within an egg-shaped structure made up of sails and rigging.

Although the official name of the work is *El nacimiento del nuevo hombre* (The Birth of the New Man), it's popularly known as the *Huevo*

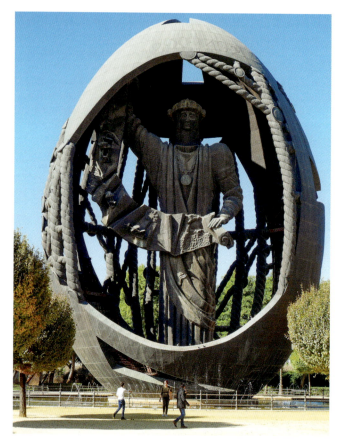

de Colón (Columbus' Egg), alluding to a legend that must surely have inspired its creator, Georgian artist Zurab Tsereteli.

The park where it stands takes its name from the nearby 16th-century monastery, and originally served as the plant nursery that supplied Expo '92. Plants would arrive here for acclimatisation from all over the world, benefiting from the park's location next to an inner harbour of the Guadalquivir in one of the river's old meanders.

The statue is the city's fourth sculptural tribute to the Genovese explorer, after the statue in the monastery of La Cartuja (1887), his tomb in the cathedral (1899) and the monument in the Murillo gardens (1921).

A scale replica donated by the sculptor is on display in the gardens of the UNESCO building in Paris.

Gift for Expo '92 not inaugurated until 1995

A gift from Moscow City Council for the 1992 Universal Exposition, the sculpture travelled from St Petersburg to the Basque port of Santurce, and carried on from there to Seville in 37 customised vehicles. The sheer size of the parts made them difficult to transport and assemble, so it wasn't installed until 1995.

Legend of Columbus' Egg

According to the Italian merchant and adventurer Girolamo Benzoni in his *History of the New World*, published in Venice in 1565, at a soirée held in honour of Columbus on returning from his first voyage, one of the nobles hosting the event commented that if he hadn't discovered the Indies it wouldn't have been long before someone else did. Columbus didn't reply, simply asking to be brought an egg. He placed it on the table and challenged his fellow diners to stand it on its tip as he would do. They all tried unsuccessfully, and when it was Columbus' turn he tapped  the egg delicately against the table, flattening its tip, and stood it upright. The marvellously simple message was not lost on any of those present: *Once a feat has been achieved and witnessed, anyone can do it.*

LEPROSERÍA DE SAN LÁZARO MOSAIC

Depiction of the beggar-saint leper on an unusual ceramic panel

Avenida del Doctor Fedriani, 56

bove the lintel of the old side entrance to San Lázaro hospital, a building located near the cemetery, there is a curious ceramic mosaic featuring the image of St Lazarus. The series of tiles is a reminder

that this hospital on the outskirts of the city was originally a leper colony.

This may be the oldest hospital institution in Spain, and has been running since it was founded in the 16th century, though some historians place it as much as three centuries earlier, during the reign of Alfonso X.

The anonymous depiction of the leprous beggar-saint, which dates from about 1760, includes all the traditional elements: the wooden crutches that signalled his presence, his ragged clothes and dogs all around him, licking at his wounds.

Leprosy was a condition that terrified the society of the day, so those afflicted by it were considered contagious and were confined to so-called 'lazarettos'. It wasn't until the 20th century that an effective course of treatment was found for this long-term bacterial infection.

From Biblical parable to Cuban Santería

Two Lazarus figures appear in the Bible, and over time popular imagination has ended up fusing them into one: St Lazarus of Bethany, the brother of Martha and Mary Magdalene, who is raised from the dead by his friend Jesus Christ, and the ulcerous beggar Lazarus, mentioned in a parable from the Gospel according to Luke. By the early 12th century this figure lent its name to the Military and Hospital Order of St Lazarus. The order was extremely active in the first crusades to the Holy Land, given over to caring for lepers while its ranks were also joined by knights from other orders who had contracted the disease.

St Lazarus underwent a further process of syncretism in Cuba, melding with the powerful African Orisha *Babalú Ayé*. In Yoruba his name meant 'Father of the Earth', and he was a deity brought to Cuba by slaves from the African continent, then transforming into the Orisha of leprosy, smallpox and venereal and contagious diseases. According to the tradition of Cuban Santería, *Babalú Ayé* was a womaniser who ended up catching leprosy, and whose wounds were licked at by dogs. Once dead he managed to come back to life, turning into a merciful figure devoted to the sick.

OUROBOROS ON THE PANTHEON ⑬ OF ISABEL PRIETO AND MIGUEL TENORIO

A tomb with mysterious symbols

Seville cemetery
Avenida Doctor Fedriani, 33
Calle Fe, left, 43
Daily 8am–5.30pm, except for 1 June–30 September 8am–4pm

On the main avenue running through Seville cemetery stands the bizarre tomb that Miguel Tenorio de Castilla commissioned in 1861 for his wife, Isabel Prieto Tirado, who died aged just 29 in the cholera epidemic that ravaged the city in 1856. This is a simple pantheon made up of a sculpted stone urn on top of a pedestal with all sorts of mysterious symbols.

The most interesting element is a relief on the pedestal featuring the circular figure of a serpent devouring itself: a so-called ouroboros (or uroboros), a Greek term that literally means 'tail-devourer'. This symbol, which was adopted by ancient alchemists and gnostic mystics, could feature a serpent or a dragon representing eternity, where there is no beginning and no end, both zero and the absolute, everything and nothing, and the natural cycle of life and death.

The serpent is curled around a relief with a winged hourglass alluding to the passage of time and the possibility of a return to the origin. The clock's compartments symbolise Heaven and Earth, which depending on man's will may be both above and below.

The urn rests on lion's claws, an Egyptian symbol used to demonstrate the virtues man should possess: courage and nobility. On the front there are some poppy buds, a symbol dating back to antiquity used to allude to the human soul and the blossoming of consciousness, and also symbolising eternal sleep.

Miguel Tenorio de Castilla was a law graduate and conservative politician born in Almonaster la Real (Huelva) in 1818. From 1859 to 1864 he served as private secretary and royal adviser to Isabella II. Historians and chroniclers from the time referred to him as her 'favourite', claiming he was the father of the Bourbon infantas Pilar, Paz and Eulalia. The fact is he retired from politics in 1880 with very little money, and moved to Nymphenburg palace in Munich (Germany), under the protection of Paz and Ludwig Ferdinand of Bavaria. He lived at the palace until his death at the end of 1916, and still lies at rest there over a hundred years later.

For more on the symbolism of the *ouroboros*, see double-page spread overleaf.

The ouroboros: a symbol of divine enlightenment

In iconography and literature the circular figure of a serpent eating its own tail can sometimes be found. The symbol is traditionally known as the 'ouroboros', a word taken from the Greek, but actually originating in Coptic and Hebrew, given that *ouro* means 'king' in Coptic and *ob* means 'snake' in Hebrew, combining to give us a 'royal serpent'. The reptile that raises its head above its body therefore serves as a symbol of mystic enlightenment. Within the framework of Hinduism it represents the sacred fire they call *kundalini*. Kundalini is how the Western medicine of the Middle Ages and Renaissance associated the bodily heat that rose from the coccyx to the cranium with the *venena bibas* (the imbibed venom spoken of by St Benedict of Nursia) of the snake whose bite is not cured with the same venom. In the same way that the Buddhist schools of spiritual enlightenment of the Dzogchen and Mahamudra reveal that the meditator should learn to 'bite his own tail like the serpent', the subject of the ouroboros and the imbibed venom remind us that spiritual enlightenment may only be attained by searching for a mental state beyond normal forms, where one looks inside oneself for true self-knowledge.

The Greeks popularised the term ouroboros in its literal sense, as 'he who eats his own tail'. They adopted this representation from the Phoenicians and Hebrews, who had in turn taken it from Egypt, where an ouroboros was depicted on a stele from as early as 1600 BCE. It represents Ra, the God of Light coming back to life from the shadows of night, which stand for death, thereby signifying the eternal return, life and death and a new start to existence. It also represents the reincarnation of the soul in successive physical bodies until it attains its optimal level of evolution, reaching bodily and spiritual perfection, an important subject for the peoples of the Orient and Middle East. As such, the snake eating its own tail may also be interpreted as an interruption in human development (represented by the serpent) to initiate the cycle of spiritual evolution (represented by the circle).

For Pythagoras it signified mathematical infinity, because the serpent as arranged in the form of a zero, an abstract number used to designate eternity, embodied in the ouroboros depicted as turning on itself.

The gnostic Christians identified it with the Holy Spirit, revealed by its wisdom as the Creator of all visible and invisible things, and whose greatest earthly expression is Christ. That's why in Greek gnostic literature this symbol is associated with the phrase '*Hen to pan*', meaning 'the all is one', and was adopted in the 4th and 5th centuries as an amulet that protected against evil spirits and venomous snakebites. This amulet was known as an Abraxas, the name of a god from the primitive gnostic pantheon which the Egyptians identified as Serapis, and it became one of the most famous talismans of the Middle Ages.

Greek alchemists were quick to adopt the figure of the ouroboros, and it even reached the hermetic philosophers of Alexandria, with whom Arab thinkers studied, introducing the image to their own schools of hermeticism and alchemy. These schools became famous, and Christians attended them in the Middle Ages. There is even historical evidence that members of the Order of the Templars, along with other Christian mystics, travelled to Cairo, Syria and even Jerusalem to be initiated in the hermetic sciences.

OUR LORD OF HONEY

A miracle or a bee colony in a cemetery?

Seville cemetery
Central junction
Daily 8am–5.30pm
1 June–30 September 8am–4pm

Acrucified Christ presides over the cemetery's central junction from the top of a stone promontory adorned with rose bushes. The late-19th-century work of local sculptor Antonio Susillo, it would later be given the suggestive nickname *Cristo de las Mieles* (Our Lord of Honey). This bizarre epithet was due to the fact that in 1940, shortly after the sculptor's remains were installed in a pantheon underneath the sculpture, honey started to seep out of Christ's bronze face. The sweet delicacy bubbled out of the crucified figure's mouth and eyes, then dripping down over his chest.

The city was thrown into uproar, with everyone wanting to see the 'miracle' with their own eyes. Finally the Church had to intervene, and emissaries are said to have been sent from the Vatican itself to clear up the matter.

Susillo was a popular and much-admired artist, the author behind iconic works that adorn squares across Seville, such as the statues of Daoiz (Plaza de la Gavidia), Velázquez (Plaza del Duque) and Miguel Mañara (Jardines de la Caridad), or the gallery of distinguished sons of the city in the palace of San Telmo (see p. 234). Sadly the artist became the victim of severe depression, apparently caused by personal, financial and professional problems, leading him to commit suicide at the age of just 41. On 22 December 1896 his body was found between the train tracks in the Barqueta area with a gunshot wound to the chin.

A ridiculous rumour quickly spread that he had taken his own life out of regret for having carved his crucified figure with Christ's feet arranged the wrong way round, with the left foot nailed to the wooden upright and the right one arranged on a little horizontal support, rather than the reverse, which is the traditional way.

It's true that Susillo's suicide meant that burial in the cemetery wasn't allowed, and it was only thanks to the pressure of influential acquaintances that permission was granted for a discreet tomb. Despite demands for

him to be given a more prominent resting place, 44 years passed before his remains were moved to beneath his famous Christ in April 1940.

As for the 'miraculous' honey, the explanation is disappointingly prosaic. Due to the great size of the bronze sculpture, Susillo had to make it hollow, with holes left for both eyes and mouth. So what better place for the cemetery's bees to install their colony during Seville's flowering spring?

MUSEO MÚSICA AFRICANA

One of the best collections of African musical instruments in the world

Calle Automoción, 16
Guided tours booked by telephone: 622 68 90 30
hola@promocionafricana.com
promocionafricana.com/proyecto/te-suena-africa

S urrounded by car workshops and builders' merchants in as unlikely
a place as an industrial park, there is a unit housing one of the best

collections of African musical instruments in existence today. Such is its importance that New York's Metropolitan Museum itself was interested in acquiring its impeccable selection.

Located at the headquarters of the Centre for African Culture, managed by the El Gulmu cultural association, the collection of more than 500 instruments is the fruit of the personal efforts stretching back more than 30 years of a pharmacist and aid worker from Cádiz called Javier Ballesteros.

The sheer range of the items on display is astonishing, whether associated with work songs, ritualistic events or celebrations, and some are more than a century old. Snakeskin drums, Kora harps whose soundboxes were enormous gourds, ritual rattles with stones, bones and shells worn on ankles or belts, string instruments with covers made from tortoise, flutes made from horn ...

Among the many eye-catching pieces is a talking drum originating from Cameroon, made using a hollowed-out tree trunk measuring almost 2 metres, and which served to communicate between neighbouring communities, announcing births, weddings, funerals and so on.

The guided tour of the exhibition, led by a musician with expertise in a vast range of instruments, covers the different sections where the instruments are arranged into four groups: chordophones (strings), aerophones (air), idiophones (where the sound is produced by the very material the instrument is made from) and membranophones (percussion instruments with stretched skin). Within each category they are arranged by country of origin, ethnicity and so on.

In addition, visitors can witness a demonstration of what some of the instruments sound like, with the recounting of legends and other curiosities, illustrating the link with modern instruments, and there is the chance to participate in an introductory workshop on African percussion music.

As a complement to its collection of instruments, the centre also houses a major repertory of African musical recordings, in addition to a curious collection of marionettes and toys from the entire continent.

ALPHABETICAL INDEX

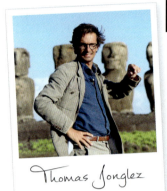

Thomas Jonglez

It was September 1995 and Thomas Jonglez was in Peshawar, the northern Pakistani city 20 kilometres from the tribal zone he was to visit a few days later. It occurred to him that he should record the hidden aspects of his native city, Paris, which he knew so well. During his seven-month trip back home from Beijing, the countries he crossed took in Tibet (entering clandestinely, hidden under blankets in an overnight bus), Iran and Kurdistan. He never took a plane but travelled by boat, train or bus, hitchhiking, cycling, on horseback or on foot, reaching Paris just in time to celebrate Christmas with the family.

On his return, he spent two fantastic years wandering the streets of the capital to gather material for his first "secret guide", written with a friend. For the next seven years he worked in the steel industry until the passion for discovery overtook him. He launched Jonglez Publishing in 2003 and moved to Venice three years later.

In 2013, in search of new adventures, the family left Venice and spent six months travelling to Brazil, via North Korea, Micronesia, the Solomon Islands, Easter Island, Peru and Bolivia. After seven years in Rio de Janeiro, he now lives in Berlin with his wife and three children.

Jonglez Publishing produces a range of titles in nine languages, released in 40 countries.

PHOTO BOOKS

Abandoned America
Abandoned Asylums
Abandoned Australia
Abandoned USSR
Abandoned Churches: Unclaimed places of worship
Abandoned cinemas of the world
Abandoned France
Abandoned Italy
Abandoned Japan
Abandoned Lebanon
Abandoned Spain
After the Final Curtain – The Fall of the American Movie Theater
After the Final Curtain – America's Abandoned Theaters
Baikonur - Vestiges of the Soviet space programme
Chernobyl's Atomic Legacy
Forbidden Places – Exploring our Abandoned Heritage Vol. 1
Forbidden Places – Exploring our Abandoned Heritage Vol. 2
Forbidden Places – Exploring our Abandoned Heritage Vol. 3
Forgotten Heritage
Oblivion
Unusual wines
Venice deserted

'SECRET' GUIDES

New York Hidden bars & restaurants
Secret Amsterdam
Secret Bali – An unusual guide
Secret Bangkok
Secret Barcelona
Secret Belfast
Secret Berlin
Secret Brighton – An unusual guide
Secret Brooklyn
Secret Brussels
Secret Buenos Aires
Secret Campania
Secret Cape Town
Secret Copenhagen
Secret Dublin – An unusual guide
Secret Edinburgh – An unusual guide
Secret Florence
Secret French Riviera
Secret Geneva
Secret Glasgow
Secret Granada
Secret Helsinki
Secret Istanbul
Secret Johannesburg
Secret Lisbon
Secret Liverpool – An unusual guide
Secret London – An unusual guide
Secret London – Unusual bars & restaurants
Secret Madrid
Secret Mexico City
Secret Milan
Secret Montreal – An unusual guide
Secret Naples
Secret New Orleans
Secret New York – An unusual guide
Secret New York – Curious activities
Secret Paris
Secret Prague
Secret Provence
Secret Rio
Secret Rome
Secret Singapore
Secret Sussex – An unusual guide
Secret Tokyo
Secret Tuscany
Secret Venice
Secret Vienna
Secret Washington D.C.
Secret York – An unusual guide

'SOUL OF' GUIDES

Soul of Athens – A guide to 30 exceptional experiences
Soul of Berlin – A guide to 30 exceptional experiences
Soul of Kyoto – A guide to 30 exceptional experiences
Soul of Lisbon – A guide to 30 exceptional experiences
Soul of Los Angeles – A guide to 30 exceptional experiences
Soul of Marrakesh – A guide to 30 exceptional experiences
Soul of New York – A guide to 30 exceptional experiences
Soul of Rome – A guide to 30 exceptional experiences
Soul of Tokyo – A guide to 30 exceptional experiences
Soul of Venice – A guide to 30 exceptional experiences

Follow us on Facebook, Instagram and Twitter

ACKNOWLEDGEMENTS

The author would like to thank all the people and institutions that have helped him in his efforts to uncover the city of Seville's hidden secrets. Without them, this encounter with the unexpected and unusual in the capital of the Guadalquivir would not have been possible.

I would especially like to thank Ángeles Hidalgo, official Seville tourist guide, for her detailed knowledge of the Cathedral and the Reales Alcázares; Daniel Jiménez Maqueda, archaeologist and historian, for introducing me to Isbiliya, Muslim Seville; Nuria Casquete de Prado, managing director of the Institución Colombina; José Almoguera, guide and graduate in history, for his knowledge of the city's Medieval Jewish quarter; Javier Peso, venerable master of Seville's Oberos de Hiram Lodge (Symbolic Grand Lodge of Spain); Antonio Ramos, lecturer in the history of pharmacy and head of the Museum of the History of Pharmacy; Colonel Alberto González Revuelta, director of the Military Museum of Seville, and the management and guides at the Seville Port Authorities.

I extend my gratitude to Martín Carlos Palomo, secretary of the Niculoso Pisano Association for the Friends of Ceramics; to Juan Antonio Pérez Tarascó, "Hermano Mayor" in the Brotherhood of San Hermenegildo; to Catalina González Melero from the Andalusian Documentation Centre for the Performing Arts; to Erika Lopez Palma, Casa de la Ciencia museum, Peruvian Pavilion (Spanish National Research Council); to Ángela Barrios Padura, tenured lecturer at the School of Architecture, University of Seville; to Álvaro Cabezas García, lecturer in history of art at the University of Córdoba; to Ricardo Alario López, lecturer at the School of Architecture, University of Seville; to Fernando Rodalva, director of CasaLa Theatre; to Amparo Graciani, professor at the School of Architecture, University of Seville; to Óscar Gil Delgado, lecturer at the School of Architecture, University of Seville; to Javier Ballesteros, director of the Museum of African Music; to Luis Aguilar, owner of the Parras Charcoal Yard, and to Manuela Santamaria.

And my particular thanks to the photographers Juan Jesús González, Anna Elías and Carmen Mateos for sharing their special glimpses of some of Seville's hidden spots. The author would also like to express his thanks to Thomas Jonglez for all of his comments and superb editorial work.

Seville's intimate charm lies in what it tells us about its past
Rubén Darío, Nicaraguan poet and diplomat (1867-1916)

PHOTOS CREDITS

All original photos are by **Ricardo de Castro**, except:
Juan Jesús González: Modernist electrical substation, Laboratorio municipal de higiene, Maquedano hat shop, Plaque on Luis Cernuda's house, Saimaza coffee roasters, Head of King Peter I, Pila del pato, Roman steles in the Giralda, Arias Correa's pillar, Hurrahs in the cathedral, Almohad patio in Casa de la Contratación, Last section of the Jewish quarter's wall, Original doorway to the Alcázar, Ceramic advert for Guadalquivir steamboats, Centro Cerámica Triana, Tomb of Diego Gómez de Ribera, Chapel of Santa María de Jesús, Relief of an indigenous Indian smoking a pipe and Pillars in the gardens of the Chilean Pavilion
Anna Elías: Moroccan Pavilion from Expo '92
Institución Colombina: Biblioteca colombina
Martín Carlos Palomo (Asociación Niculoso Pisano): Tombstone of Íñigo López
Álvaro Cabezas García: Ordeals of Diego Duro
Carmen Mateos: Hungarian Pavilion from Expo '92
Macu Anelo: Biography of the author

Map of the Jewish Quarter in Seville (p. 179) based on the one published by Gil, O. (2013)
"A synagogue uncovered in Seville: architectural study", *Sefarad*, vol. 73:1

Cartography: Cyrille Suss – **Design:** Emmanuelle Willard Toulemonde – **Translation:** Dan Whitcombe – **Editing:** Jana Gough and Caroline Lawrence – **Proofreading:** Kimberly Bess – **Publishing:** Clémence Mathé

© JONGLEZ 2022
Registration of copyright: March 2022 – Edition: 01
ISBN: 978-2-36195-549-6
Printed in Bulgaria by Dedrax